THE KINGFISHER ENCYCLOPEDIA

OF THE FUTURE

THE KINGFISHER ENCYCLOPEDIA

OF THE FUTURE

KING*f*ISHER

NEW YORK

Authors
Anthony Wilson, Clive Gifford

Senior Editor
Clive Wilson

Deputy Art Director
Mike Buckley

Designer
Veneta Altham

DTP Coordinator
Nicky Studdart

Production Controller
Jacquie Horner, Caroline Jackson

Picture Research Manager
Jane Lambert

Picture Researcher
Juliet Duff

Indexer
Hilary Bird

KINGFISHER
Larousse Kingfisher Chambers Inc.
95 Madison Avenue
New York, New York 10016

First published in 2001
1 3 5 7 9 10 8 6 4 2
1TR/0400/TWP/RNB(RNB)/135NMA

LIBRARY OF CONGRESS CATALOGING-IN-PUBLICATION DATA
has been applied for.

ISBN 0-7534-5360-6

Printed in Singapore

CONTENTS

INTRODUCTION

During the 21st century, we will witness great changes in our lives. Breakthroughs in fields as diverse as medicine, communications, and transportation will have a major impact on society.

New technologies will continue to power the Information Revolution. The next generation of microprocessors and virtual reality systems will have far-reaching effects on the way we communicate, learn, and work. Machines will become smarter and more powerful. Robot carers will look after the sick, while tiny robots will perform delicate surgery deep inside the body. Advances in health care and medicine will lead to a significant increase in life expectancy, and one day gene therapy may even be able to prevent most life-threatening diseases.

Most people will live in cities, which will go on growing outward and upward. Inside your intelligent home, sensors will detect your presence and automatically adjust the environment. If you own a car, it will probably be a non-polluting electric model. For longer journeys, new forms of propulsion will cut the journey times for train, sea, and air travel.

Some of the predictions made in this book may never happen, and others will come sooner or later than predicted. But one thing is for certain—whatever our future has in store, it will be an exciting time to be alive.

2200?
Human brain, connected to microchips, able to survive outside body

2060?
Intelligent computers built using "neural net" technology

2050?
Many factories totally automated

2050?
Microchips with ten trillion transistors become available

2025?
Computers speak, listen, and have other senses

2020?
"Flexiviewer" computer developed to fit in pocket

2020?
Cars drive themselves on main roads

2010?
First billion-transistor chip

1977
Personal computers (PC) sold in stores

"When five computers have been sold, the world won't need any more," predicted the head of the computer firm IBM in the 1940s. Since then, computers have developed from simple number crunchers to powerful multipurpose information and communication machines that have revolutionized the way we live—and in the late 1990s, computers were selling at the rate of five every second. In the last fifty years, they have also increased in power an astonishing ten billion times. In the next half century, computers will continue to develop at a phenomenal rate, doubling in power every eighteen months. When they have their own sense systems and the ability to learn, they will begin to reason more like humans, becoming self-aware and learning from their mistakes. Computers will be everywhere, working away, often invisibly, inside every machine and gadget. By 2020, in the world's more developed countries, it is estimated that there could be as many as a hundred times more computers than people.

LIVING WITH COMPUTERS

1971
Pocket calculators go on sale

1970
First microprocessor made

1958
First integrated circuit

1947
Transistor invented

1940s
First electronic computers built in Britain and the U.S.

1834
Babbage plans a mechanical computer

AGE OF THE MICROPROCESSOR

In the time it takes to say "microprocessor," half a billion new transistors are made in factories around the world. Transistors are tiny electric switches, some so small that you need a microscope to see them. Huge numbers of them can be linked together to make complex circuits called microprocessors.

Microprocessors, also called microchips, are probably the most important invention of the last five centuries. Computers, televisions, telephones, and other electrical equipment in homes, cars, offices, and factories all rely on microchips to function—without them our lives would be very different. And without microchips none of the changes predicted in this book could ever happen.

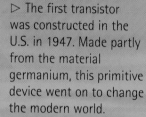

△ Early transistors were small enough to make portable radios a reality in the early 1950s. By the 1970s, most transistors were built into microchips.

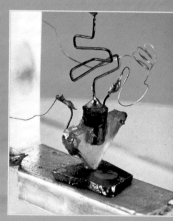

▷ The first transistor was constructed in the U.S. in 1947. Made partly from the material germanium, this primitive device went on to change the modern world.

△ During the 1960s, computers like the IBM 702 filled a large room. They were prone to frequent breakdowns and had much less computing power than today's home computers.

▷ Microchips flooded onto the market during the 1970s, after new techniques made it possible to manufacture ready-wired circuits, containing tiny transistors and other components, in a single process.

"The day the future began"

On December 23, 1947, three American scientists demonstrated the world's first transistor, built from a paperclip, gold foil, and a slab of shiny material called germanium. Fifty years later, transistors outnumbered humans by a million to one. In fact, there could be at least ten million of these tiny switches in your home at this moment. Before transistors were available, radios, televisions, and computers used much larger electric valves. If one of today's digital phones used valves in place of transistors, it would be as big as a skyscraper.

▽ A typical computer contains a microprocessor and a number of other silicon chips. Each chip does a particular job and contains thousands of switching devices, or transistors. Wires called "feet" connect the chips to the computer.

Miniaturization

As transistors become smaller, microprocessors become more powerful. By 2010, transistors will be so small that 2,000 of them will fit across the width of a single human hair. Billion-transistor microchips will be common, and computers will come on a single microchip. According to the man who invented the microprocessor, Federico Faggin, microchips containing ten trillion transistors will be available by 2050.

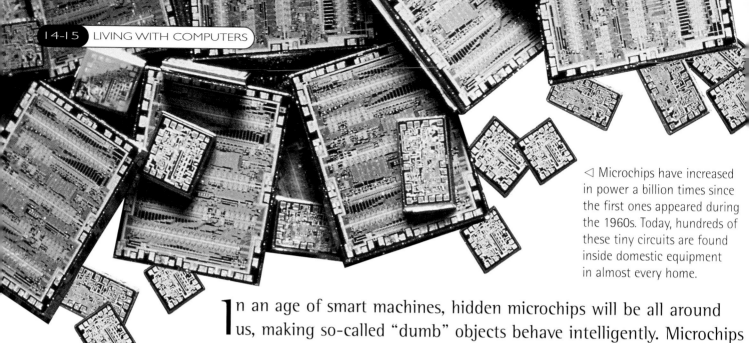

◁ Microchips have increased in power a billion times since the first ones appeared during the 1960s. Today, hundreds of these tiny circuits are found inside domestic equipment in almost every home.

In an age of smart machines, hidden microchips will be all around us, making so-called "dumb" objects behave intelligently. Microchips will be embedded in all kinds of devices and everyday objects from cars to food packaging. Ovens will "know" what they are cooking, and buildings that require maintenance will

CHIPS WITH EVERYTHING

alert engineers automatically. Smart cards—like credit cards but with a microchip inside—will be commonplace, communicating by radio with the external world. Personally coded so that no one else can use them, smart cards will open locked doors, carry data such as medical records, and, of course, be used instead of cash.

△▷ Although inefficient and difficult to operate, this vacuum cleaner from 1910 was an exciting novelty. Its microchip-controlled successor in the 21st century will no longer require human help to keep the house clean.

Sensing the world

Sensors are the key to the intelligent future. These miniature devices will come in many different forms and connect computers and other machines to the outside world. Using tiny microphones, machines will recognize voices and sounds. Mini video cameras and radar will enable machines to "see" their surroundings and navigate around obstacles, while infrared sensors will monitor human movement by body heat.

▽ Microchip-powered controls and indicators inside a cockpit enable pilots to land an aircraft safely in the dark.

> Intelligent buildings, such as this Japanese museum, can adapt to changing conditions, automatically switching from solar energy to conventional sources when necessary.

At home

Kitchen equipment first showed signs of becoming "smart" as long ago as the 1930s, when ovens were first equipped with thermostats and a little later with automatic timers. However, many of these devices were often complicated to use and they frequently malfunctioned. Advances in microchip technology will continue to make most household machines and gadgets much more efficient and user-friendly.

Saving the planet

Smarter homes mean a cleaner, greener environment. Improved microchip controls for lighting and heating will save energy, while a proposed intelligent garbage can will crush garbage, remove its smell, and sort it into different materials for recycling. All new cars will be fitted with automatic controls that fine tune the engine to reduce pollution and ensure that every drop of energy is extracted from the fuel.

BLURRED VISION

▷ Intelligent devices will perform many different tasks in the home by 2020. Robots will serve drinks to guests, and therapy beds will provide massage and other treatments.

A climate-controlled yard keeps winter at bay in this house of the future, designed during the 1950s. Building costs have prevented such proposals from seeing the light of day.

COMPUTERS IN CONTROL

△ Robby the Robot caught the public imagination in the 1956 movie *Forbidden Planet*. Karel Čapek adopted the term "robot" in 1920. It comes from a Czech word meaning "forced labor."

When a new computer-controlled luggage handling system was tested at Denver International Airport in 1994, chaos ensued. Automatic carts crashed into walls, and bags were taken to all the wrong places. The problem was traced to a bug—a human error in the instructions given to the computer. This incident demonstrated that intelligent machines still have serious limitations.

The breakthrough will come by 2010, when computer-controlled machines will be intelligent enough to learn from their own mistakes and find a way around any bugs in their software. Smart machines will be found not just in airports, but also in hospitals, shopping malls, factories, garages, and in our homes.

this one may go into production by
...r design ensures perfect streamlining
...iency.

...st fully-automated factories
...hat lies ahead. Working 24 hours
...ormed complex tasks, such as
...micals for drug manufacturers or
...ing TV sets and cellular phones.
...ns were nowhere to be seen, apart
...one or two highly skilled engineers
...d to oversee the computers and
...achines in case anything went
wrong. By 2050, the majority
of factories will be like this.

◁ Architects and designers rely
on computers to help them visualize
complex, three-dimensional structures,
such as these factories. In the future,
computers will also have a role in
building and testing as well as design.

Danger zones

In 1979, the robot Rover 1 helped prevent a major
catastrophe when it was sent in to repair the damaged
nuclear reactor at Three Mile Island. As computer power
increases, robots will take over more and more tasks
from humans in dangerous places—whether it is in
a nuclear reactor, on the ocean floor, or in a raging
forest fire. With laser-guided bombs and pilotless
fighter planes, some future wars will be fought between
advanced computer systems—watched over by human
controllers far from the battle zone.

◁ Robot welders
became a familiar
sight in car factories
in the 1980s. Robots
perform best when
doing repetitive jobs.

▷ During the 1991
Gulf War, automated
bombs homed in with
pinpoint accuracy on
targets picked out by
laser beams.

Beyond our planet

Robot craft have already traveled much farther
into space than humans. Early space explorers
included the two Viking landers, sent to Mars
in the 1970s. In 1997, the robot rover Sojourner
spent three months analyzing rocks on Mars.
By 2010, it is expected that robot explorers will
bring back dust from a comet and visit Pluto,
the outermost planet in the solar system.

CRYSTAL
BALL

As robots become more intelligent and
versatile, they will reach the point where they
begin to design and build improved versions
of themselves. Some futurists predict that
by 2100, robots may have even become the
most intelligent form of life on earth.

USING COMPUTERS

Today, most home computers are still deaf, dumb, and blind—unable to sense, let alone react, to the outside world. But by the 2020s, computers will be able to interact fully with their users. They will recognize our gestures, detect our body heat, and carry out voice commands. They will even be able to monitor our health and alert a doctor if they think we need one.

Advances in light-emitting display (LED) technology will allow computers to have thin, flexible screens that roll out like a blind. As the cost of computers continues to fall, they will be as common—and as disposable—as sheets of paper. And with improved software, home computers will become truly user-friendly, diagnosing and fixing their own problems.

△ Desktop machines like the iMac, which first appeared in 1998, are much easier to use than their predecessors. It is designed for instant, one-button Internet access.

▷ A century before electronic calculators were developed, Charles Babbage designed his mechanical "calculating engine"—but it was never completed. This portion alone contains 2,000 precision-made parts.

The cost of living

In the last twenty years, the cost of computing has come down a thousand times, while the power of a home computer—the number of "operations" it can do every second—has increased by a similar amount. If cars had improved as much as computers, a family car would now be as powerful as a jet fighter plane and cost less than the price of a compact disc.

▷ Supercomputers, such as the CM-5, contain 1,000 or more processors all working together—compared to the single one used in a normal desktop computer. Computing power on this scale is needed for complex tasks such as weather forecasting.

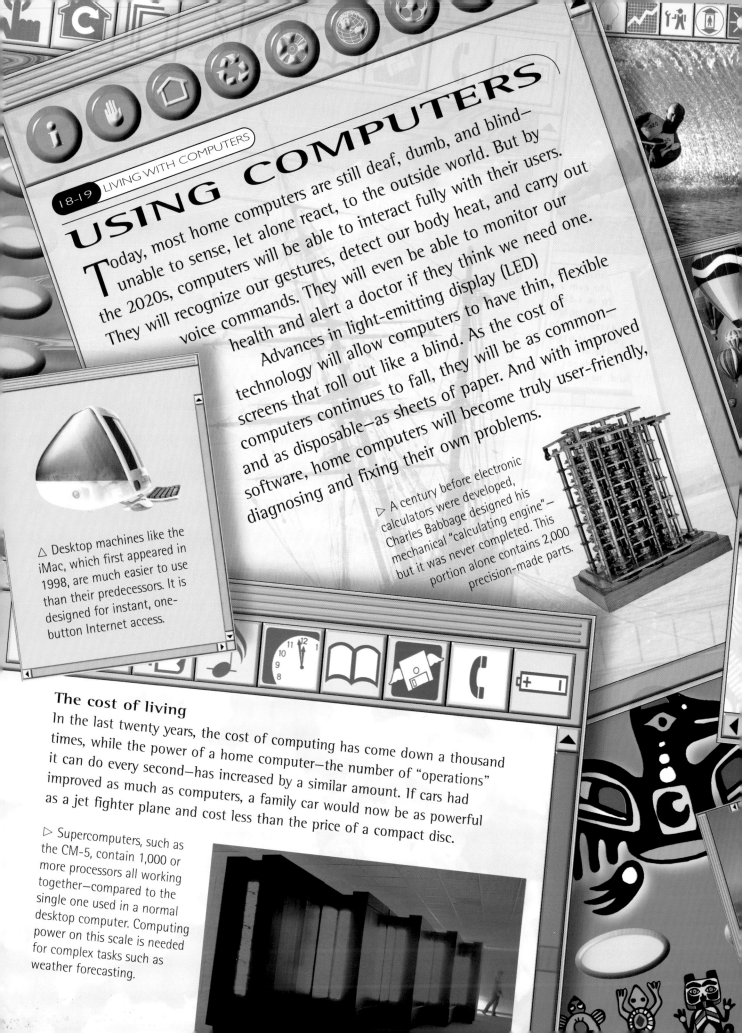

◁ A large color display will be the main feature of this "flexiviewer" personal communicator predicted for the year 2020. The magazine-sized screen scrolls down to fit in a pocket when not in use.

One box for all

Forty years ago, the first commercial computers were slow number crunchers, mostly used for solving numerical problems. With no keyboard or screen, they were far harder to communicate with than today's more powerful computers. However, with videophone, television, and the Internet built into one portable unit, personal computers will become even more versatile, as well as smaller and faster than current machines.

◁ By 2005, lightweight, portable computers will be voice-controlled and recognize handwriting. A solar-powered microphone and earpiece (*below*) will be linked to the main unit by radio.

△ By 2050, home computers may resemble sheets of paper —thin, flexible screens with a microchip inside. They will come in tear-off pads and will be widely available. A radio link will connect them to a central processor and to the Internet.

Light beams and particles

By 2010, high-powered computers will work so quickly—one quadrillion calculations a second—that wire connections will be useless. Only light rays will move fast enough to carry data inside these "optical" machines. By 2050, quantum computers will use and manipulate subatomic particles. These will solve in seconds problems that can take years of work by today's supercomputers.

▷ Cybercafés, where machines are available to rent, provide low-cost Internet access and the chance to communicate with people from around the world.

HANDLING INFORMATION

Before we reach the year 2010, it will be possible to pack all of the information in a library of 2,000 books onto a single microchip no larger than your thumbnail. Retrieving data from this billion-byte memory chip will take only a few millionths of a second. Today's limited and sluggish computer storage systems, such as magnetic disks and CD-ROMs, will be a distant memory. Information can be stored on the Internet, too. To help us navigate through the vast and ever-expanding sea of data, we will depend on "intelligent agents." These digital assistants will learn our needs and automatically search the Internet for relevant information.

▷ For nearly 2,000 years, books have been vital for storing and providing information. Before printing was invented, handwritten books were rare and treasured possessions.

Photographic memory

Fifty years ago, the first computers had tiny memories that stored no more than a thousand bytes. Today, a home computer stores millions times more than this in its internal memory chips and hard disk. Silicon chips might be succeeded by holographic memories. These will pack hundreds of billions of bytes into tiny patterns in layers of photographic film. By 2020, a single holographic memory unit will be able to hold as much data as all the world's computers did in 1998.

△ The greater part of human knowledge is stored in libraries around the world. People have kept written records in one form or another for over 5,500 years.

CRYSTAL BALL

By 2200, the human brain may be kept alive without any body at all, connected instead to microchips, artificial senses, and other support systems. Such a being might live forever—or until someone else decided to switch it off.

Today's computers store information in electronic boxes—to retrieve the data you simply open the right box. But pioneers are developing new memory systems that work like the human brain, where memories are stored by association, each memory connected to many similar ones. Ultimately, these memory chips may be linked directly to our brains.

△ Writing was the earliest way of preserving knowledge other than in our heads. These ancient Egyptian hieroglyphs, or picture signs, were carved in stone just over 3,000 years ago.

▷ In the 1990s, CD-ROMs became a very important storage system. A single disk can store the equivalent of 50 million words.

The book

One essential way to store and share ideas and information has remained popular for more than 500 years. It is the technology in front of you now—a printed book. In the future, many books and magazines will be downloaded from the Internet, but printed matter is unlikely to be completely replaced.

▷ Intelligent agents called "knowbots" will not only filter specific information from the Internet, but also assess whether it comes from a reliable source. A human face makes the agent more user-friendly.

◁ Until the 1850s, quill pens were the main method of putting words on paper by hand. The quill was cut from a wing feather, often from a goose or swan.

△ Before printing was invented in the 1450s, books were produced by scribes, often working in monasteries, who copied them by hand.

WORKING
WITH WORDS

In 1990, a prize of $100,000 was offered to the first person who could design and build a computer that could think for itself. To date, no machine has succeeded in winning.

For years, computers have worked with words typed in letter by letter. Their ability to recognize spoken words—and to speak for themselves—will soon make keyboards a thing of the past. But it will probably not be until 2050 that computers develop artificial intelligence (AI) and can understand the words they handle. By 2100, computers may be able to think as effectively as humans and even develop consciousness, becoming the first machines that actually know they are machines.

◁ In the 1950s, office secretaries relied on manual typewriters. Editing and correcting mistakes became much easier when word processors arrived in the 1970s.

Answering back
Computers that recognize human speech are widely available. Software that can recognize up to 40,000 words can be used for dictation with over 95 percent accuracy. Increasingly, computers will not only listen, but also talk back. Computer expert systems already exist that offer specific advice on subjects such as interpreting a medical X ray or filling in a tax form.

Improving efficiency

In the late 20th century, millions of jobs disappeared as powerful computers were used to handle words and figures automatically, working much faster than humans can. For people who still have jobs, computers that talk and listen will help them work much more efficiently. In 2020, it has been estimated that people in some jobs will achieve as much in a month as their parents could in a whole year.

Human role model

Today, most computers can only do one thing at a time, but they do it extremely fast. Human brains are much slower, but can do many things at once, using a network of billions of neuron nerve cells. Some experts believe that computers will only begin to become really intelligent some time after 2050, when they, too, are made of neural nets—the electronic version of our own brain cells.

◁ Calligraphy—the art of beautiful writing—is still highly valued in China. Chinese characters and the techniques for drawing them have changed little in the past 4,000 years.

▷ The human brain contains a network of at least ten billion special cells called neurons. By 2050, computers may rely on networks of electronic neurons.

▽ A new generation of "neural net" computers, which mimic the way the human brain works, would finally enable machines to translate text and spoken words from one language to another as effectively as humans.

blando más despacio

1965
First communications satellite relays 240 phone calls at once

1956
First telephone cable under the Atlantic

1930s
All five continents linked by radiotelephone

1901
Marconi sends first radio messages across the Atlantic

1876
Bell invents the telephone

1837
First public demonstration of telegraph

2015?
Holophone projects lifelike 3-D images

2010?
Most homes have fiber-optic link to the outside world

2008?
Personal communicator combines computer, videophone, and Internet access in one portable unit

2005?
Children allocated a personal number they keep for life

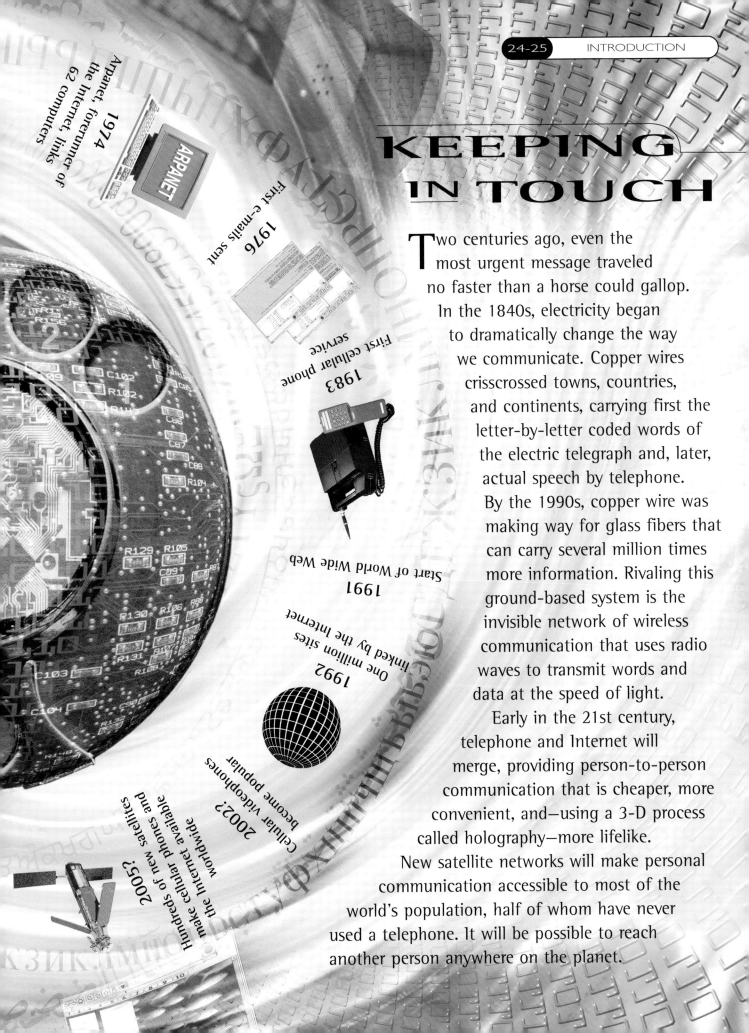

KEEPING IN TOUCH

Two centuries ago, even the most urgent message traveled no faster than a horse could gallop. In the 1840s, electricity began to dramatically change the way we communicate. Copper wires crisscrossed towns, countries, and continents, carrying first the letter-by-letter coded words of the electric telegraph and, later, actual speech by telephone.

By the 1990s, copper wire was making way for glass fibers that can carry several million times more information. Rivaling this ground-based system is the invisible network of wireless communication that uses radio waves to transmit words and data at the speed of light.

Early in the 21st century, telephone and Internet will merge, providing person-to-person communication that is cheaper, more convenient, and—using a 3-D process called holography—more lifelike.

New satellite networks will make personal communication accessible to most of the world's population, half of whom have never used a telephone. It will be possible to reach another person anywhere on the planet.

1974
Arpanet, the forerunner of the Internet, 62 computers, links

ARPANET

1976
First e-mails sent

1983
First cellular phone service

1991
Start of World Wide Web

1992
One million sites linked by the Internet

2002?
Cellular videophones become popular

2005?
Hundreds of new satellites make cellular phones and the Internet available worldwide

IT'S GOOD TO TALK

It has been estimated that people born in the year 2000 will spend more than two years on the telephone during their lifetimes. Yet when the first telephones came into use during the 1870s, many people doubted whether the invention would catch on.

The telephone will continue to change our lives as the new century progresses. By 2010, cellular phones will work in most places on the planet, while automatic switching between fiber-optic and radio networks will provide high quality and inexpensive links to the global network. Children will get their own phone number as soon as they can speak, and keep the same number all their lives.

Making history

In 1876, the invention of the telephone by Alexander Graham Bell, a Scotsman who settled in the United States, marked the beginning of modern telecommunications. The first words picked up by his assistant in another room were "Mr. Watson, come here. I want you." In October that year, they held the first long-distance telephone conversation between Boston and Cambridge, Massachusetts—a distance of nearly two miles (3km). By 1880, there were more than 70,000 subscribers to the new telephone service.

△ Until the invention of the telephone, the telegraph was the only way of sending long-distance messages rapidly.

▽ Alexander Graham Bell's 1876 telephone used separate devices for receiver and mouthpiece. At first, the general public showed little interest in his invention.

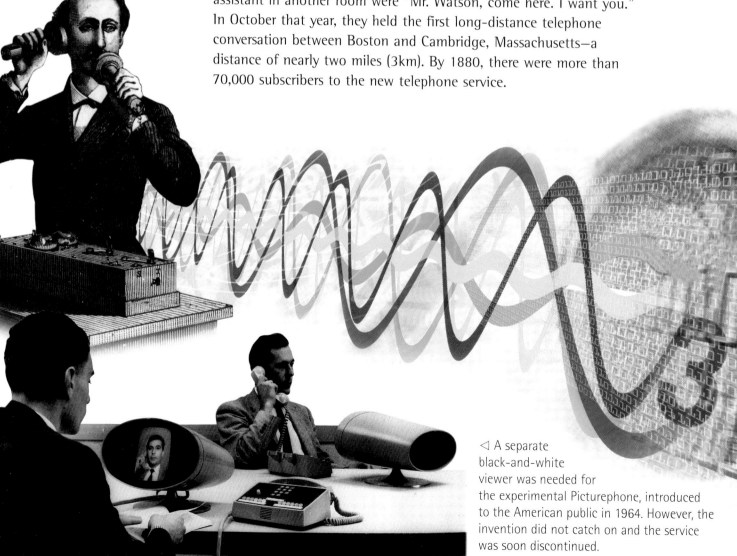

◁ A separate black-and-white viewer was needed for the experimental Picturephone, introduced to the American public in 1964. However, the invention did not catch on and the service was soon discontinued.

◁▽ Upright telephones gave way to the more familiar cradle version in the 1930s. Another innovation, the dial, brought a faster service for callers.

△ As well as conventional telephone calls, the dataphone, planned for 2005, allows images, text, and other visual data to be viewed on a small detachable eyepiece.

Full circle

The first messages sent by telegraph down electric wires used an early version of digital technology—each letter of the alphabet was coded into a pattern of short and long beeps. For many years after this, the telephone used an analog system where sound vibrations are converted into electrical vibrations and then back again. Today, we are heading for an all-digital future, when telephone messages (and radio and television broadcasts) are converted into a series of digits (zeros and ones). Digital transmission means more data can be sent down a single cable without becoming distorted.

Innovations

The shift to all-digital technology is driving advances in communication devices. Cellular phones, for example, are becoming smaller and more cost-effective; by 2005, videophones will transmit and receive high-quality images as well as high-fidelity sound.

▽ The changeover from analog to digital transmission, in which speech is coded into pulses made up of zeros and ones, will continue to bring better sound quality, cheaper calls, and new services for telephone users.

LINKED BY LASER

During the 1980s, an invisible revolution took place in the way we communicate. Laser light, passing down long, thin strands of glass called optical fibers, began to replace electricity and copper wires as the best way to carry telephone messages. By 1988, a single fiber-optic cable under the Atlantic Ocean was carrying 40,000 telephone conversations at the same time. By 2020, most homes in affluent countries will be joined to the communications network by two-way fiber-optic links, carrying high-quality sound and video for phones, multichannel television and radio, and other information services.

△ Early steamships were used to lay telegraph cables across the ocean floor. By 1874, all five continents were linked.

Crystal clear

Overhead phone wires, looping from poles to houses, have been part of the scenery for more than a century. Now they are disappearing fast, replaced by underground cables that carry glass fibers as thin as an eyelash. The glass is so clear that, in theory, it would be possible to see through a window made from it that was over 60 miles (100km) thick.

▽▷ Optical fibers, carrying thousands of phone calls down a single glass strand, have largely replaced overhead cables, which needed one wire for every phone call made.

◁ The first laser was made by American physicist Theodore Maiman in 1960. Laser stands for light amplification by stimulated emission of radiation. Laser light travels in an intense, narrow beam.

Pulses of light

The laser is a vital 20th century invention that will drive the communications network of the 21st century. Lasers used in communications supply a narrow beam of ultrapure infrared light. This can be emitted through fiber optics as a stream of tiny flashes. Because the laser can flash so fast—up to one trillion times a second—its beam can carry vast amounts of information. In fact, you could download all the pictures and words in a thousand books like this one in less than a second.

▷ Today, lasers are used not just in communications, but as laboratory tools, in CD players, bar-code readers, microsurgery, and in industry. The most powerful lasers can cut through metal and other materials.

△ The transmission of people through space, or teleportation, will still be impossible by 2015, but the holographic telephone will be the next best thing. Holophones will use lasers to re-create in real time a realistic 3-D image of the person at the other end of the line.

Avoiding bottlenecks

Traditional copper cable is known as a "narrowband" channel. It can only carry a limited amount of information. Fiber optics is "broadband"—it can transmit up to one hundred times the amount of information. However, to cope with the increasing speed and amount of data, the electronic switches at the receiving end will also have to be replaced by switches that are made from lasers.

▷ Individual strands of pure glass, many miles in length but much thinner than a human hair, are the backbone of modern communications. Coded pulses of laser light travel along each strand.

LOOK, NO WIRES!

▽ At just over 1,840 feet (553m), Toronto's CN Tower is the tallest freestanding structure in the world and a vital link in Canada's radio communications network.

In 1912, one feeble radio message saved hundreds of lives. It was sent by the radio operator of the doomed ocean liner *Titanic* and was picked up by another ship close enough to rescue 700 passengers. Today, a similar type of "wire-less" communication is used by anyone who has a cellular phone. Radio waves, traveling through the air at the speed of light, relay messages between the phone and the nearest receiving tower or passing satellite.

By 2010, radio communication will be common inside homes and offices, too. The familiar tangle of cables that connect computers, printers, and other devices will disappear as more and more equipment becomes cordless, and data is sent and received instead by short-range radio links.

△ Wireless telegraphy, or radio, was first developed by the Italian scientist Guglielmo Marconi. He transmitted a message across his father's estate, and used a flat metal plate as his receiving antenna.

Wireless world

Until the 1890s, long-distance communication— either by telegraph or by telephone—was restricted to places that were connected by electric wires. Then, in 1895, Guglielmo Marconi succeeded in sending telegraph code signals through the air over a distance of about one mile. He soon discovered that the higher the receiving antenna, the greater the signals' range. In 1901, Marconi sent a radio message from Europe to the U.S., and soon millions of radio messages were flashing around the world every day.

BLURRED VISION

The personal radio receiver was predicted in 1909, half a century before transistors made miniature radios a reality. A frock coat and top hat were essential pieces of the equipment, carrying antenna and power supply respectively.

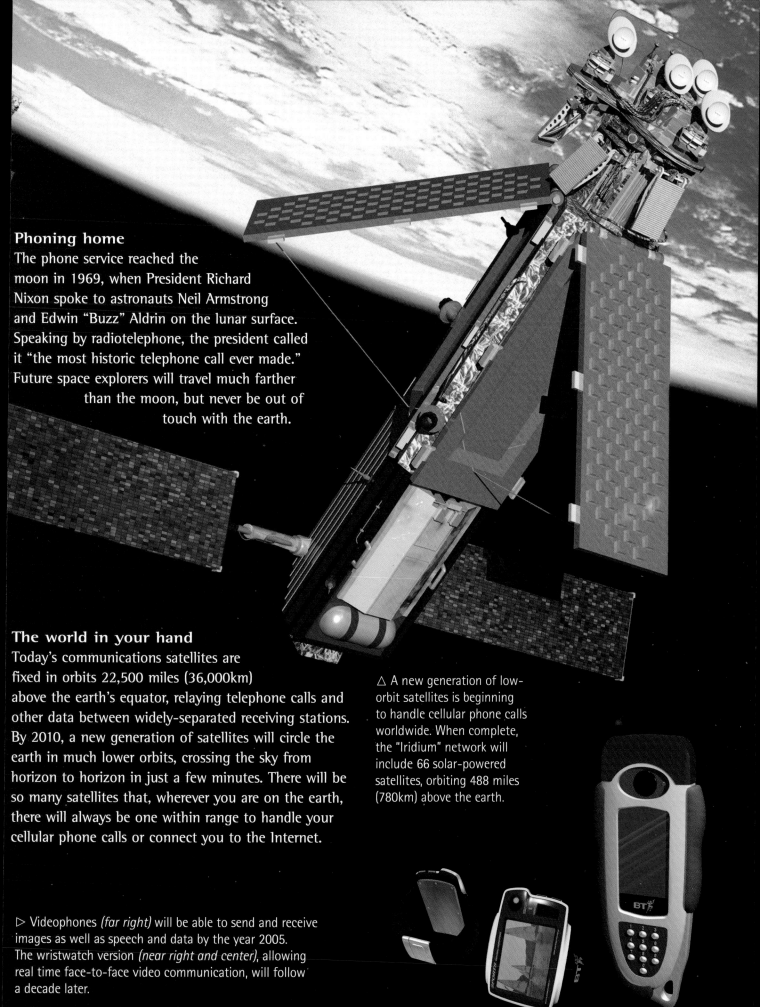

Phoning home

The phone service reached the
moon in 1969, when President Richard
Nixon spoke to astronauts Neil Armstrong
and Edwin "Buzz" Aldrin on the lunar surface.
Speaking by radiotelephone, the president called
it "the most historic telephone call ever made."
Future space explorers will travel much farther
than the moon, but never be out of
touch with the earth.

The world in your hand

Today's communications satellites are
fixed in orbits 22,500 miles (36,000km)
above the earth's equator, relaying telephone calls and
other data between widely-separated receiving stations.
By 2010, a new generation of satellites will circle the
earth in much lower orbits, crossing the sky from
horizon to horizon in just a few minutes. There will be
so many satellites that, wherever you are on the earth,
there will always be one within range to handle your
cellular phone calls or connect you to the Internet.

△ A new generation of low-
orbit satellites is beginning
to handle cellular phone calls
worldwide. When complete,
the "Iridium" network will
include 66 solar-powered
satellites, orbiting 488 miles
(780km) above the earth.

▷ Videophones (far right) will be able to send and receive
images as well as speech and data by the year 2005.
The wristwatch version (near right and center), allowing
real time face-to-face video communication, will follow
a decade later.

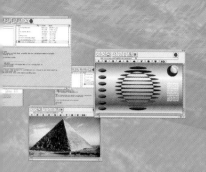

Less an information superhighway than a bad case of gridlock has been many people's experience of the Internet during the 1990s. But by 2010, the early years of the Internet will be long forgotten. Broadband fiber-optic connections will bring a new high-speed Internet directly into homes and offices, with access so rapid that tasks like downloading an entire movie will take only a second or two. Fleets of new satellites will make this superNet accessible anywhere on earth.

CAUGHT IN THE NET

Using miniature portable communicators, more than a billion enthusiasts around the world will rely on the Internet for information and entertainment as well as for business and personal communication.

◁ Tim Berners-Lee, a British mathematician, invented the system of linking one site to another that has made the World Wide Web so popular.

Going global

Computers worked in isolation from one another until 1961 when engineers in California succeeded in establishing a communications link between two machines. Soon, a telephone-based network of computers was developed in great secrecy. This network would function as an effective means of communication, even in the event of nuclear war. By the early 1990s, this system, known as Arpanet, had mushroomed into a vast global network of a million computers and was renamed the Internet.

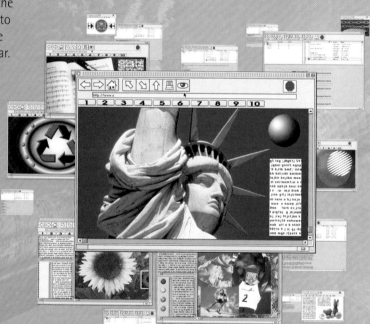

△ At first, websites—the "home pages" of organizations and people who use the Internet—only carried words, but pictures soon followed. In the future, broadband Internet will add high-quality sound, video, and many other features.

◁ During the 1960s, military officials at the Pentagon in Washington, DC planned a new communication system that would allow scientists to contact each other after a nuclear war. The Internet eventually emerged from this system.

Sending packets

One of the keys to the Internet's success is packet switching. Data is broken up into sections, each of which makes its own way through the Internet to the destination. There, another computer reassembles the original message. Packet switching makes the best use of the Internet's capacity, and it bypasses parts of the Internet that may be overloaded or out of action.

Spreading its net

The Internet will evolve in many different ways. It is already replacing more conventional ways of communicating, such as writing letters, publishing books and magazines, or simply pinning up notices on a bulletin board. Many experts believe the Internet will soon carry the world's telephone calls and much of its television and radio broadcasting, too.

△ A dense network of fiber optics provides the backbone of the Internet. Satellites now bring Internet by radio to people on the move and to parts of the globe that fiber optics cannot reach.

◁ The Internet's vital linking stations operate night and day. This one is in the high-security Telehouse building in London, England.

2010?
Miniature memory cards store music

2005?
Satellites bring high-quality radio broadcasting to developing countries

1998
Digital broadcasting introduced

1997
Deep Blue, a computer, beats Gary Kasparov, world chess champion

1982
CDs begin replacing phonograph records

1975
VCRs become widely available

ENTERTAINMENT

Since the 1980s, millions of computers around the world have been designed and sold for one thing only—playing games. Videogame computers are only the latest in a long line of inventions that have included photography and movies, radio and television, the phonograph, personal stereos, CD players, and VCRs. All of these devices have one thing in common—they are designed to keep people entertained in their spare time.

Today, low-cost digital equipment allows ordinary people to produce sounds and images that once required specialized equipment that had to be operated by experts. Digital technology will revolutionize broadcasting. There will be thousands of television channels to choose from—plus countless new Internet television and radio stations. If that is not enough, then the next generation of high-quality virtual reality systems should keep you occupied and entertained!

1962 Telstar satellite relays first television pictures between Europe and the U.S.

1949 Over a million people own television sets in the U.S.

1922 More than 500 radio stations operating in the U.S.

1920 Millions of people have phonographs

1895 Lumière brothers show first motion picture

1888 Kodak camera invented

VIRTUAL WORLDS

Since prehistoric times, humans have sometimes wanted to escape everyday reality and to transport themselves to new worlds. Today, using virtual reality technology, you can instantly immerse yourself in a computer-generated environment. Special headsets and data gloves give the impression of being inside an imaginary place in which you can move, float, or even fly.

By 2015, bodysuits packed with sensors and feedback devices will be widely available. With computers controlling the input to all the senses—taste and smell, as well as sight, sound, touch, and movement—users will experience entirely believable virtual worlds, from taking part in a historical battle to visiting another planet.

Beyond fun and games

Games and entertainment are major driving forces in the development of virtual reality technology. But it also has serious uses, such as the practice of delicate operations by surgeons or the training of fighter pilots. Scientists are also taking advantage of virtual reality. By manipulating virtual molecules, for example, they can begin to create new materials or learn about highly complex structures.

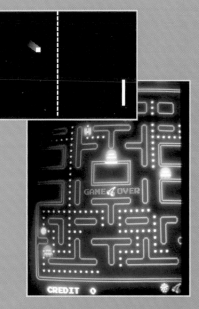

△ Commercial computer games first appeared in the 1970s. Although the graphics were crude, they were an introduction to computers for many people.

△ Coin-operated pinball machines became popular in arcades around the 1950s, but computerized arcade games began to replace them thirty years later.

Creating life

For many years, scientists have explored the way living things change and evolve by "breeding" digital life-forms in computers. Like real organisms, these electronic versions live, reproduce, and eventually die. As software develops, more intelligent forms of so-called Artificial Life will appear, spreading worldwide through the Internet. In the 21st century, advances in Artificial Life will lead to a new generation of computers that can learn, evolve, and even repair themselves.

△ A huge range of increasingly sophisticated games is available to players. Since the 1970s, computer games have developed into a hugely profitable and competitive industry with a global market.

Face the fear

Virtual spiders have already been used to cure people who have arachnophobia, an uncontrollable fear of real spiders. Wearing virtual reality headsets, these people can overcome their terror by being introduced to virtual spiders that gradually increase in size. In the 21st century, virtual reality will help people overcome many other fears and worries that prevent them from leading normal lives.

△ Advanced mechanical sytems linked to powerful computers provide realistic simulations of anything from Formula 1 racing to interstellar combat.

▷ A virtual reality station of 2015 will immerse the user's whole body in computer-generated sensations that completely replace the real world.

△ Norns, Grendels, and other virtual creatures are born, live, and die inside the computers that run the latest Artificial Life games. Scientists use similar software to learn how biological-based life-forms evolve and interact.

◁ Virtual reality headsets will be standard equipment in many homes. Their uses will range from entertainment to training and "conditioning"—helping the wearer overcome psychological difficulties and phobias, such as fear of spiders.

△ The first sound recording was made by the American inventor Thomas Edison in 1877. His phonograph originally stored sound on a cylinder covered with tinfoil.

ELECTRONIC ARTS

In 1997, an American orchestra gave the first performance of Mozart's 42nd Symphony—even though Mozart only wrote 41 symphonies and had been dead for more than 200 years. The new symphony was the work of a computer, aided by a human composer who programmed the machine to write in the style of Mozart.

During the 21st century, more and more of the music we hear will be written and performed by computers. Paintings and sculptures created by computers may become commonplace, too. However, until computers have the capacity to feel and express emotions, it is doubtful whether computer art and music can ever match, let alone surpass, the best works created by humans.

△ Digital technology records and recreates the work of composers and artists in high-definition sound and vision. In the 21st century, computers will be able to create original art and music.

▷ From vinyl records to digital tapes, recording quality has improved dramatically over the last fifty years.

Master disks

The first phonograph records could only play three minutes of music and had to be made one at a time. If one hundred copies were needed, the musician had to perform the same piece one hundred times! A century later, double-sided DVDs (Digital Versatile Discs) can store two hours of high-quality sound and video, and are produced in factories that stamp them out by the millions.

△ Early phonographs used a needle to pick up vibrations from grooves in the record and fed them into the speaker horn.

△ One DVD can store as much data—sound or vision—as a million phonograph records from the 1920s.

Playback time

By 2010, instead of buying prerecorded disks, we will be able to download music (as well as movies) straight from the Internet. Memory cards no bigger than a postage stamp will store the music. These will be inserted into playback systems the size and thickness of a credit card. Today's personal stereos and CD and DVD players will be seen only in museums, alongside old-fashioned phonographs.

△ In a modern recording studio, digital technology allows engineers to enhance recorded tracks in many different ways. Their creative input can be as important as that of the original performers.

◁ By 2015, 3–D holographic sculptures will be a centerpiece in many homes.

Noise pollution

As the world becomes a noisier place, an electronic sound system known as Active Noise Control will become an increasingly important feature of our lives. By creating sound waves that cancel out unwanted noise, Active Noise Control can create a pool of silence around you.

THE MOVING IMAGE

At the beginning of the 21st century, one hundred years after the birth of movies, computer-generated digital effects—from asteroids to talking pigs—have became commonplace. Electronic movie stars have even replaced flesh-and-blood actors. When every frame of a film is a computer-processed image, new digital stars can be created, and old ones—such as Charlie Chaplin or Elvis Presley—can be brought back to life to feature in new productions. You may even get a chance to appear on the big screen yourself, in a personalized digital edition of your favorite movie.

△ The 1902 movie *A Trip to the Moon* was one of the first to use models and special effects. The French director George Méliès adapted tricks he had learned as a stage magician.

From film to chip

For 150 years after its invention in the 1839, photography was a chemical process. Still pictures were mostly recorded on film, which had to be developed and printed in special laboratories. In the 1990s, digital cameras became commercially available. These do not require film. Instead they capture the image on a special microchip, ready to be viewed on a computer or television screen. For moving images, handheld camcorders first appeared in the 1980s, recording onto standard magnetic videotape, but by the late 1990s, digital movie cameras were beginning to replace these.

△ Special glasses allowed audiences in the 1950s to watch films in 3-D. Smell-O-Vision was another innovation of the period.

▽ Video technology provides one alternative to more traditional movie screens. This giant video wall in Poitiers, France, is made up of 850 high-definition screens.

△ In the 1880s, Eadweard Muybridge used a device called a zoopraxiscope to project images of moving animals and people. The pictures were taken with 24 still cameras arranged in a row.

True to life

When color holographic video becomes available, we will at last be able to see films in ultrarealistic 3-D, instead of on a flat screen. Holography is a complex process that mixes light beams to re-create the true appearance of solid objects. Primitive holographic video has been demonstrated by Professor Stephen Benton at the Massachusetts Institute of Technology's Media Laboratory, but we will probably have to wait until after 2010 before the quality is good enough for general use.

△ Ordinary people will become movie stars, too, when digital techniques allow a person's image to be seamlessly integrated with the on-screen action. Holography will add the extra drama of three-dimensional imagery to these personalized movies.

TUNING IN

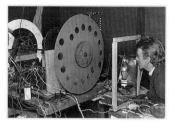

△ John Logie Baird successfully demonstrated television in the 1920s, using a large spinning disk to scan the image.

In the early days of television in the 1930s, there were reports of viewers dressing up in their best clothes. They believed that if they could see people on the screen, then the people on the screen could see them! By 2010, television really will be a two-way experience. An interactive television may not actually watch you all the time, but it will soon learn your viewing preferences and suggest programs of interest from the thousands of channels on offer. You will even be able to select your own camera angles for watching a football game, choose items to build up news reports, and give instant feedback on programs.

▷ The Freeplay radio is ideal for places with no electricity or where batteries are hard to obtain. Winding it up powers the set for 25 minutes.

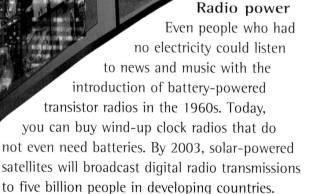

Radio power

Even people who had no electricity could listen to news and music with the introduction of battery-powered transistor radios in the 1960s. Today, you can buy wind-up clock radios that do not even need batteries. By 2003, solar-powered satellites will broadcast digital radio transmissions to five billion people in developing countries.

△ Digital radios will combine more channels and CD-quality sound with new facilities such as touch-screen displays and the ability to record programs.

▽ Hang-on-the-wall televisions first appeared in the late 1990s, when full-color, flatscreen plasma displays began to displace the much bulkier, vacuum-tube screens used for the past 60 years.

Box of tricks

By 1998, some computers could receive television signals, and some digital televisions could be connected to the Internet. This marked the beginning of the merging of computers and television. By 2005, the telecomputer will be a feature of many homes. Television, radio, and a full Internet service will be available in a single unit.

▽ Floor-to-ceiling video screens may replace conventional walls and windows by 2020. A range of programs to suit the viewer will be selected automatically from the countless channels available.

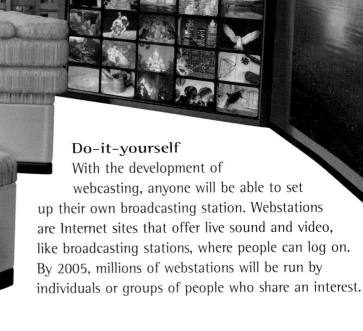

Do-it-yourself

With the development of webcasting, anyone will be able to set up their own broadcasting station. Webstations are Internet sites that offer live sound and video, like broadcasting stations, where people can log on. By 2005, millions of webstations will be run by individuals or groups of people who share an interest.

Hamburger Abendblatt

Freitag, 19.30 MEZ = Tatort Dallas in Texas

Kennedy ermordet

Kopfschuß aus
dem Hinterhalt

Frau Kennedy
blieb unverletzt

Johnson neuer
US-Präsident

2025?
Medi-beds monitor health
and alert doctors

2020?
Four out of ten workers
based at home

1920s
Phone system links millions of homes to outside world

1971
Open University begins in Britain—Students learn via TV

1997
Internet bookstores lead the way in online shopping

2003?
100 million computers are linked by the Internet

2007?
Online customized shopping for many items

2010?
People use Internet to vote in elections

2010?
Children around the world educated from home

2010?
Electronic communication centers in many homes

2015?
Most banking done on Internet

THE WORLD IN YOUR HOME

It took nearly a century for the number of telephones in the world to grow from one to a hundred million. By 2003, the number of computers on the Internet will have grown that much in just ten years, and the Internet will continue to expand faster than ever.

The Internet will link our homes to the outside world in all kinds of new ways, handling not only telephone and television, but a host of other activities including shopping, voting, and banking. Increasingly, people will learn and work from home, and even contact their doctor and be diagnosed via the Internet. Machines and domestic gadgets will be on the Net—cars, for example, will send an e-mail to their owners when they need maintenance. By 2020, in the world's richer countries at least, the broadband Internet will be an essential part of life. Like the air we breathe, we will use it all the time without even thinking about it.

GLOBAL VILLAGE

When Admiral Nelson was killed in the Battle of Trafalgar in 1805, it took two weeks for the news to reach the papers in Britain. But when Diana, Princess of Wales, died after a late night car crash in Paris in 1997, a billion people around the world knew about it just a few hours later.

News travels fast in the modern world. In the 21st century, the nerve center of many homes will be the communications center. The communications center will not only receive the news, but will also be used for entertainment, education, or simply catching up with distant friends.

△ The Crimean War of the 1850s was the first in which the public was kept informed regularly of events. News reports were telegraphed back home and appeared in the papers the following day.

Shrinking world

Two hundred years ago, many people never ventured more than a few miles away from home. They had little contact with the outside world. In the 20th century, newspapers, radio, and television have given people a window on the world from their own homes. Since the mid-1990s, the Internet has been turning the world into a true "electronic village." Finding out what is happening thousands of miles away is just a matter of switching on your computer.

△ Radio news bulletins were a lifeline for families in Europe during World War II. Transmissions were often interrupted by fading sound and interference.

Personal service

By 2007, news will not be restricted to bulletins at fixed times. You will be able to specify what you want as well as when you want it—whether it is local or national news, or something of more personal interest, such as the progress of a favorite sports team or stocks and shares. The computer will download specific items, compiling your own personal news bulletin.

▽▷ The communications center will be a major feature of future homes, with personalized news from near and far always available.

▷ When President John F. Kennedy was assassinated in November 1963, the news was broadcast to millions of people around the world.

▽ Images of our planet taken by satellites and spacecraft have underlined the fact that we are all part of a single global community.

Politics and power

By 2010, in many countries, presidents and governments will be elected by people voting from home on the Internet. Frequent referendums will give everyone a chance to vote on important decisions affecting their country or neighborhood. Some governments will use the Internet to inform people of how much tax to pay and transfer the money directly from their bank accounts.

ONLINE HOME

For most people, access to the Internet will mean a whole new range of services. Electronic shopping already exists, and many products, from books to airline tickets, can be bought over the Internet. With the introduction of electronic cash that can be used globally and personalized goods delivered directly from the manufacturer, conventional shopping will steadily decrease. It is estimated that by 2010, 20 percent of purchases will be made using the Internet.

Services other than shopping will also be available online. Possibilities include people in one country consulting medical experts in another country about their health, or farmers in remote areas downloading satellite pictures that provide information about their crops and livestock.

△ Supermarkets appeared in major cities during the 1950s and 1960s. Their main attraction was low prices and the novelty of selecting and handling goods yourself.

Consumer choice

In the 21st century, customization—personalizing products according to the specifications of buyers—will increasingly replace mass production. Using your computer, you will link up directly to the factories that make clothes, cars, and other products. A user-friendly interface will enable you to select colors, shapes, and other design features. If you want new clothes, lasers will scan your body to calculate the exact size. Finally, the finished product will be delivered directly to your door.

▽ A wide choice of on-line shopping is already available on the Internet. Choosing travel destinations, buying clothes, and ordering flowers are just a few of the many services.

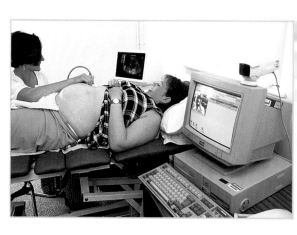

△ Using a video link and the Internet, a doctor studies the ultrasound scan of a pregnant woman at her local clinic, located many miles away.

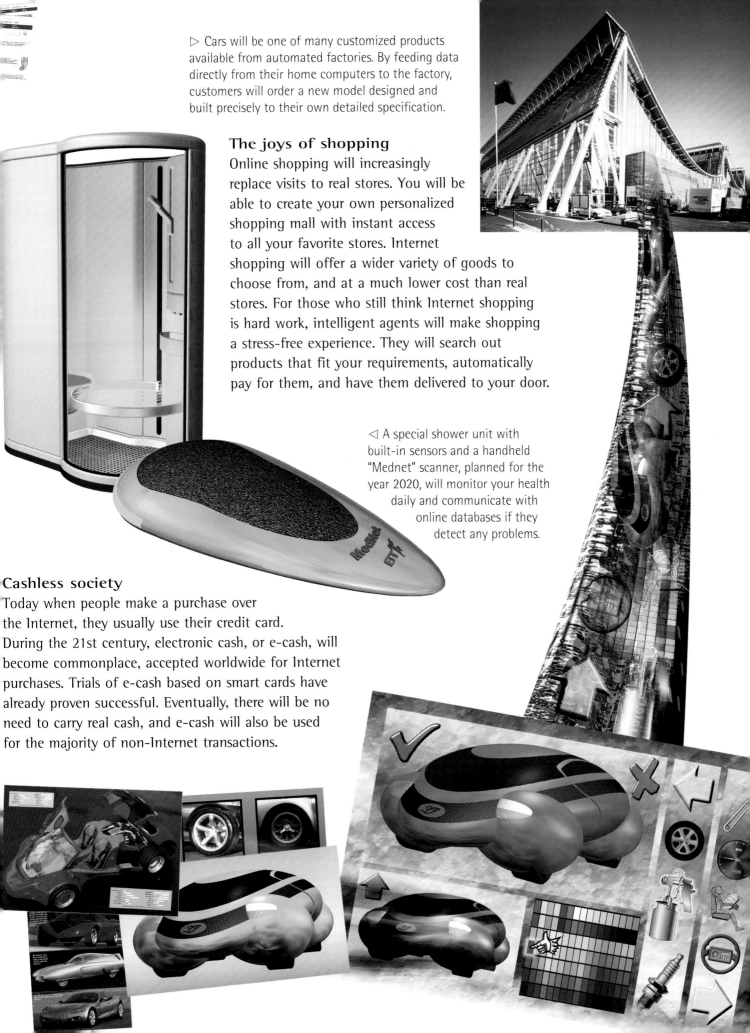

▷ Cars will be one of many customized products available from automated factories. By feeding data directly from their home computers to the factory, customers will order a new model designed and built precisely to their own detailed specification.

The joys of shopping

Online shopping will increasingly replace visits to real stores. You will be able to create your own personalized shopping mall with instant access to all your favorite stores. Internet shopping will offer a wider variety of goods to choose from, and at a much lower cost than real stores. For those who still think Internet shopping is hard work, intelligent agents will make shopping a stress-free experience. They will search out products that fit your requirements, automatically pay for them, and have them delivered to your door.

◁ A special shower unit with built-in sensors and a handheld "Mednet" scanner, planned for the year 2020, will monitor your health daily and communicate with online databases if they detect any problems.

Cashless society

Today when people make a purchase over the Internet, they usually use their credit card. During the 21st century, electronic cash, or e-cash, will become commonplace, accepted worldwide for Internet purchases. Trials of e-cash based on smart cards have already proven successful. Eventually, there will be no need to carry real cash, and e-cash will also be used for the majority of non-Internet transactions.

▷ It has been calculated that people who worked in cities during the 1990s spent the equivalent of three whole years of their lives battling rush hour on their way to and from work.

◁ Before the development of factories in Europe during the 1700s, whole families worked together at home making cloth and other products.

WORKING AT HOME

By 2020, four people in ten will be working from home instead of an office. Designers, architects, software engineers, and many others who use computers will no longer need to commute to work. These "telecommuters" will use the Internet and high-capacity optical links to keep in touch with their employers and clients, who may be in distant parts of the world. Telecommuting eliminates the need for the majority of a company's employees to assemble in a specific place each day. For those who miss the social aspects of the workplace, local centers will be set up where they can meet other workers.

△ During the 21st century, people such as architects will no longer gather in a single workplace. Instead they will be based at home, working together as a team linked by the Internet and other communication devices.

Teamwork

Whenever a new cathedral was built in the Middle Ages, craftsmen, such as stonemasons and carpenters, frequently traveled from distant parts of the country to work on the project. During the 21st century, a similar system will operate. To design a new aircraft, for example, highly skilled professionals, such as engineers and programmers, will form a team. But they will rarely meet one another. They will be linked instead by computer and will operate from their own workstations around the world.

Career prospects

In the 20th century, many people kept the same job for life. But by 2010, the idea of a long-term job will no longer be valid. Instead of taking a permanent job, many people will work on a succession of different projects. Computers and robots will continue to take over repetitive, manual jobs previously performed by humans—in banks and factories, for example. But new technologies will also create many new opportunities, such as in the entertainment and software industries.

△ Architects and engineers working in different countries pooled their resources to design one of the masterpieces of late 20th-century architecture. The Guggenheim Museum in Bilbao, Spain, was built using advanced technology and high-tech materials such as titanium.

Job satisfaction

Telecommuting will result in increased productivity and improved morale as people will be able to spend more time with their families. Another related benefit will be a reduction in pollution caused by rush hour traffic. Telecommuting will not only transform our working practices, it will also affect where we live. We will no longer need to be based near or in big cities and future telecommuters will set up new communities wherever they wish.

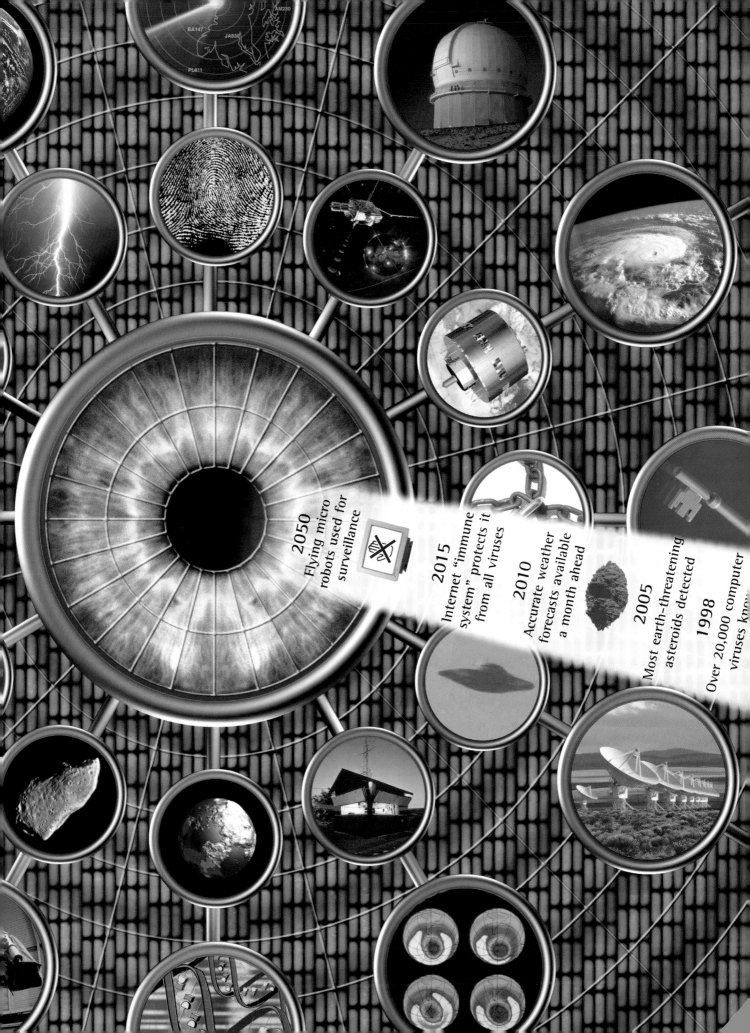

2050
Flying micro
robots used for
surveillance

2015
Internet "immune
system" protects it
from all viruses

2010
Accurate weather
forecasts available
a month ahead

2005
Most earth-threatening
asteroids detected

1998
Over 20,000 computer
viruses know...

KEEPING WATCH

When Tony Bullimore, a British yachtsman, was trapped under the hull of his capsized boat in the Antarctic Ocean in 1997, his life was saved by space-age communications. An automatic beacon on his yacht sent out a radio signal that was picked up by a passing satellite and relayed to a control center in France. From there, an Australian ship was alerted to rescue him.

During the 21st century, the microchip will help make life safer for many more people on the planet. In our homes, detectors and robot systems will warn us of dangers and automatically take action. Satellite positioning systems will mean that you will never get lost wherever you are in the world, and other satellites will give early warnings of hurricanes and earthquakes. Even the possibility of a devastating impact from space will be reduced by powerful hardware designed to detect and destroy asteroids.

1990s
Security cameras appear across many cities

1968
First clear photos of earth taken from space

1930s
Weather ballons first sent to probe upper atmosphere

A.D. 132
In China, device invented for detecting earthquakes

HOMEWATCH

Today, millions of people depend on electronic intruder alarms and smoke detectors to feel safe in their homes. By 2020, many new homes will have intelligent security systems, connected by radio to a wide range of sensors hidden around the building. As well as detecting intruders and the first signs of smoke, a computerized system will monitor air and water pollution and warn of harmful bacteria in the kitchen and other dangers around the house. The main system will be linked to a community system for extra security or to protect your home while you are away.

△ More than 2,000 years ago, the Romans used geese, which cackle loudly when disturbed, as an alarm system to warn them of an enemy invasion.

Unlocking doors

Keyless locks will be common in the 21st century, opening doors automatically when the right person approaches. Computers will use biometric technology to identify people. Some systems will scan and recognize a person by their voice or their face. Others will recognize fingerprints, the patterns on the iris of an eye, or even identify our DNA makeup—the genetic code that is unique to each one of us.

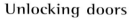

◁▷ Losing your key will soon be a thing of the past. Advanced recognition systems will automatically scan your DNA, fingerprints, or irises, and only open doors to those who have been authorized.

Ideal home

Smart homes will not only recognize us, but automatically respond to an individual's needs. Once a person has been identified—either by biometrics or a wearable microchip—the computer will operate a range of devices such as lights, heaters, air-conditioning, and even other computers. The intelligent building of 2020 will also be able to learn, remembering, for example, the user's preferences for lighting levels and room temperature.

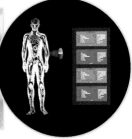

△ In 1998, Professor Kevin Warwick of Reading University in England had a small glass tube containing a microchip sewn into his arm. It allowed him to interact with his building, which opened doors for him and kept track of his movements.

Crime fighting

Microchips that allow devices to work only in the house for which they are purchased will be one deterrent to burglars in the 21st century. If items are taken, they will send out a radio signal that can be tracked by the police. Internet crime and viruses may pose more of a challenge to security services. Criminal hackers and crime syndicates already use the Internet to gain access to secret information or illegally transfer money.

△ The Internet provides a breeding ground for computer viruses to wreak havoc on machines. An effective immune system that protects the Internet will be in operation by the second decade of the 21st century.

SR2 CYBERGUARD

WARNING

△ This robot guard is used in buildings to detect fire, steam, and gases. It uses video cameras and has temperature, smoke, and humidity sensors.

△ By 2005, affordable miniature video cameras will be widely available. People will be able to use these cable-free devices anywhere in the home.

CRYSTAL BALL

By 2050, insect-sized flying robots called bugbots could be in use, equipped with tiny cameras to send back pictures to a remote monitor. Fleets of bugbots will act as mobile security cameras. In the home, they could be used to watch over a baby.

SPYING AND DEFENSE

Ever since wars began, opposing sides have attempted to find out as much as they can about the enemy's position, size, and weaponry. Spying has always involved sending human scouts and agents behind enemy lines. However, the future is likely to see unmanned machines taking over, with human operatives safely conducting surveillance operations from a distance, using computer networks. Advances in information technology will mean that a person's actions on the Internet and other networks can be traced easily. By 2010, electronic tagging with minitransmitters may also allow people to be tracked accurately without their knowledge.

△▽ Cameras have long been used for spying, often hidden in household items or miniaturized to make them harder to detect. Advances in microengineering will continue to shrink the size of radios, bugs, and cameras— the tools of the spy's trade.

Stealth

"See, but do not be seen" is a motto for all spies, especially for the pilots of spy and reconnaissance aircraft that fly over enemy territory. Stealth technology is designed to confuse enemy radar and other sensors, allowing aircraft to fly undetected. Featuring radar-absorbing paints, angled facets, and low-heat emitting engines, this technology is being improved for the second generation of stealth planes and is also being adapted to land and sea vehicles.

△ Spy movies, like the James Bond series, tend to show agents who operate alone. In reality, many spies work in close contact with their controllers.

△▷ The minimum size of an object seen from a spy satellite is known as its resolution. Current satellites are believed to have a resolution of about 20 inches (8cm). Future models will be able to read over a person's shoulder, if they are not already capable of doing so.

Spies in the sky

Despite the effectiveness of stealth technology, pilots and crew will continue to be at risk. One viable alternative is automated, computer-controlled pilotless aircraft. Pilotless drones have already been used for some routine duties, but as computer control becomes more sophisticated, unmanned aerial vehicles (UAVs) will fly more and more missions over enemy territory. By 2015, many reconnaissance and spying flights will be performed by UAVs.

Spying from space

It is no secret that many of the satellites orbiting earth are used for spying. What is secret, however, is the definition and quality of the images. The results that the public sees are probably not the very best that intelligence agencies can obtain. Satellites are used because they provide relatively risk-free information gathering. However, this may not always be the case. NASA and the Pentagon are currently spending $50 million a year developing anti-spy satellite devices.

△ The Lockheed B2 bomber has a stealth flying wing design covered in radar-absorbing material. This allows it to fly deep into enemy territory without detection.

◁ Everything a spy needs to conduct video surveillance can be contained in a briefcase. Remote-operated machines may perform this sort of surveillance task by 2020.

◁ This ingenious earthquake detector was invented by a Chinese scientist nearly 2,000 years ago. Tremors dislodged a small ball from the central container into the mouth of one of the waiting frogs.

EARTHWATCH

Satellites have transformed the way we study our planet. In a few orbits, a satellite can provide a detailed survey of a remote or mountainous area that would take years to map from the ground. By 2005, more than 30 "Earthwatch" satellites will be studying the earth from space. Some will check on weather systems and ocean currents, while others will measure air pollution, detect floods and forest fires, and keep watch for ships illegally discharging oil into the sea. It will also be possible to buy images of any point on the earth's surface, showing details as small as three feet across or less.

Weather report

Before the launch of the first weather satellite in 1960, forecasts were based on just a few measurements from balloons and ground stations. By 2010, satellites and more computer power will make detailed 30-day forecasts possible. Effective ways of changing the weather will also be developed, such as treating clouds to prevent dangerous hailstorms from developing. By 2050, huge wind barriers could be in use to alter wind patterns and control the climate in various parts of the world.

△ *Explorer II* was one of the first balloons used by scientists to carry instruments into the upper atmosphere. In 1935, it reached an altitude of 13 miles (22km) and took the first photographs that clearly showed that the earth's surface is curved.

◁△ A hurricane's distinctive swirling cloud pattern, 600 miles (1,000km) across, is easily spotted from space. For people on the ground, it can bring torrential rain and winds up to 155 mph (250km/h).

Spaceship earth

In the 1960s, the first photographs of the earth taken from space dramatically changed the way we relate to our world. They made people realize that we live on a fragile, precious planet. With this came a new awareness about our responsibility to safeguard the environment. By 2020, it should be clear whether humans are winning the battle to preserve the earth for future generations, or whether we are heading for a global catastrophe caused by pollution and the climate changes it produces.

▽▷ Bridges and buildings collapsed in the Kobe earthquake in Japan in 1995. A satellite image shows ground movements after a major earthquake.

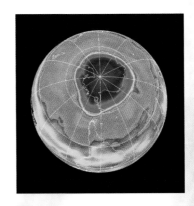

Tremors

By 2025, according to some experts, it will be possible to predict exactly when earthquakes and other natural disasters are going to happen. It might even be possible to prevent some of the more devastating effects caused by them. Scientists, for example, may be able to stop earthquakes by pumping water into faultlines to prevent potentially catastrophic stresses from building up.

▷ The ozone hole over Antarctica stands out vividly in a false-color satellite image. The ozone layer, which protects the earth from the sun's ultraviolet rays, has been damaged by chemicals called chlorofluorocarbons (CFCs), which were once commonly found in aerosol spray cans.

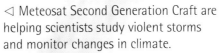

◁ Meteosat Second Generation Craft are helping scientists study violent storms and monitor changes in climate.

△ In 1908, a huge fireball flattened over 1,000 square miles (3000 sq km) near Tunguska, Siberia. Scientists believe it was caused when part of a comet exploded.

SPACEWATCH

▽ A new generation of optical telescopes is helping astronomers study how planets form around distant stars. The Very Large Telescope in Chile has a mirror 26 feet (8m) across.

In December 1997, a twelve-billion-year journey through space finally came to an end when light rays traveling from the most distant galaxy yet detected reached the world's largest telescope in Hawaii. It was one of many spectacular discoveries that astronomers have made by attaching supersensitive electronic eyes called CCDs (Charge-Coupled Devices) to their telescopes. In the years ahead, second-generation space telescopes and giant earth-based instruments will reveal even more about the origin and structure of the universe. Closer to home, automated telescopes are already watching out for asteroids that threaten our safety on earth. Another search, for signs of extraterrestrial life, will also be aided by increasingly powerful electronics.

▷ In 1965, Arno Penzias and Robert Wilson discovered radio waves left over from the Big Bang—the event that created the universe. They used a radio antenna that was orginally designed to pick up signals from the *Telstar* satellite.

Earth under threat

Scientists are concerned that there are thousands of near-earth asteroids—space rocks hefty enough to cause catastrophic damage if they collide with the earth. By 2005, computerized telescopes will have tracked down the most threatening ones, so that possible impacts can be predicted well in advance. But the main challenge is to develop ways of using rockets or lasers to break up asteroids far out in space, or nudge them into orbits that take them out of earth's path.

△ As part of the search for extraterrestrial intelligence, the world's largest radio telescope, at Arecibo, Puerto Rico, sent out a coded signal in 1974.

▽ A plaque on the Voyager 1 spacecraft carries a message from the earth describing who we are to any aliens who might intercept it.

Moon base

By 2050, a powerful transmitting station, built on the far side of the moon, could beam out messages by radio and high-powered laser to possible civilizations in distant parts of our galaxy. The station would run unmanned for many years, powered by its own nuclear reactor.

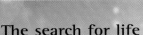

◁ Many science fiction movies have featured attacks by unfriendly aliens. In this 1953 poster for *War of the Worlds*, terrified humans flee Martian invaders.

The search for life

Many astronomers believe that the first step in detecting extraterrestrial intelligence is to locate planets orbiting distant stars. Imaging these planets is extremely difficult because they are small and dim, hidden in the glare of their local stars. There are proposals for arrays of space telescopes to be positioned near Jupiter, well away from dust in the inner solar system. These would be able to see planets directly as they orbit other stars. They might even be able to detect gases such as water vapor and ozone, suggesting a friendly climate and the existence of life.

△ High-energy lasers offer one possibility of preventing a catastrophic asteroid impact. Heat from the lasers vaporizes the asteroid's surface, causing it to give off jets of gas. These jets act like rockets, deflecting the asteroid away from earth.

1970s
Use of composite materials, e.g. in fighter aircraft

1960s
Early development of smart materials

1961
First industrial robot, built by Unimation

1908
First mass production assembly line

1903
Development of stainless steel

1767
Spinning jenny first machine to spin many threads at a time

1728
Falcon's loom uses punch card system

MACHINES IN INDUSTRY

People have been using machines ever since the first prehistoric human scraped an animal hide with a sharpened flint edge, or moved a large rock with a stick as a lever. Machines have developed in complexity as we have learned how to use and control aspects of the world around us—from making and shaping materials, such as metals, to manipulating forces, such as electricity and air pressure.

The 20th century saw a revolution in the way many people work. Much of that is because of machines, from the rise of mass production in factories with its dependence on machines and automation, to the invention of the computer, which has transformed millions of jobs. In the future, humans will supervise robots and automated machine workers, often from far away, as the remote, automated factory becomes a reality. With giant leaps in nanotechnology and microengineering, communications technology and new materials, the products of the future may not only be very different from today's, but may also be manufactured in completely new ways.

1988
First use of robots in
nuclear power plants

1990s
First molecular
machines designed

2006
Smart metal alloys used
for domestic objects

2008
Fully dextrous
multipurpose robot in use

2015
VR and automation
allow customization via
remote factories

2060
Nanorobots used in
surgery

ROBOTS AT WORK

Although there are currently thousands of robots at work all over the world, robotics—the study, design, and improvement of robots—is still in its infancy. Even so, many robots perform tasks that are impossible for humans and do some jobs more quickly and accurately than us. However, developments in robotics are expected to happen, creating far more flexible, versatile, and affordable machines that will be able to work with little or no human intervention. Whatever the speed of development, one thing is certain—our dependence on robots is only going to increase as we move further into the 21st century.

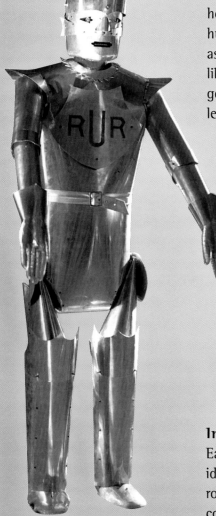

△ Automatons, like this model carriage, are machines that simulate realistic activity.

What is a robot?

There is not one perfect definition of a robot. It is fair to say, however, that it is an automated machine that performs some humanlike actions and reacts to certain external events, as well as to preprogrammed instructions. A robot does not have to look like a human. Robots are designed for a specific job. If a robot is going to work in only one place, for example, it does not need legs or a system to move around.

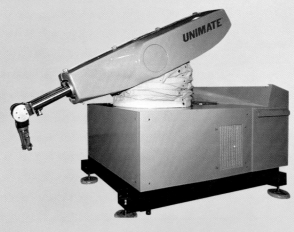

△ The Unimate robot is a direct descendant of the very first robot arm—a machine that first handled hot metal die-casting in 1961.

△ The word "robot" featured in a 1922 play called *Rossum's Universal Robots,* by Karel Čapek. It comes from the Czech word meaning "forced labor."

Intelligent glimmers

Early robots were extremely good at repeating an identical operation time after time. New generations of robots, equipped with high-resolution vision systems and complex object recognition, will be able to adjust and adapt to a greater range of work scenarios. By 2030, robots are likely to be equipped with advanced "fuzzy logic" circuits. These will help them make decisions in keeping with the complexities and problems of the real world.

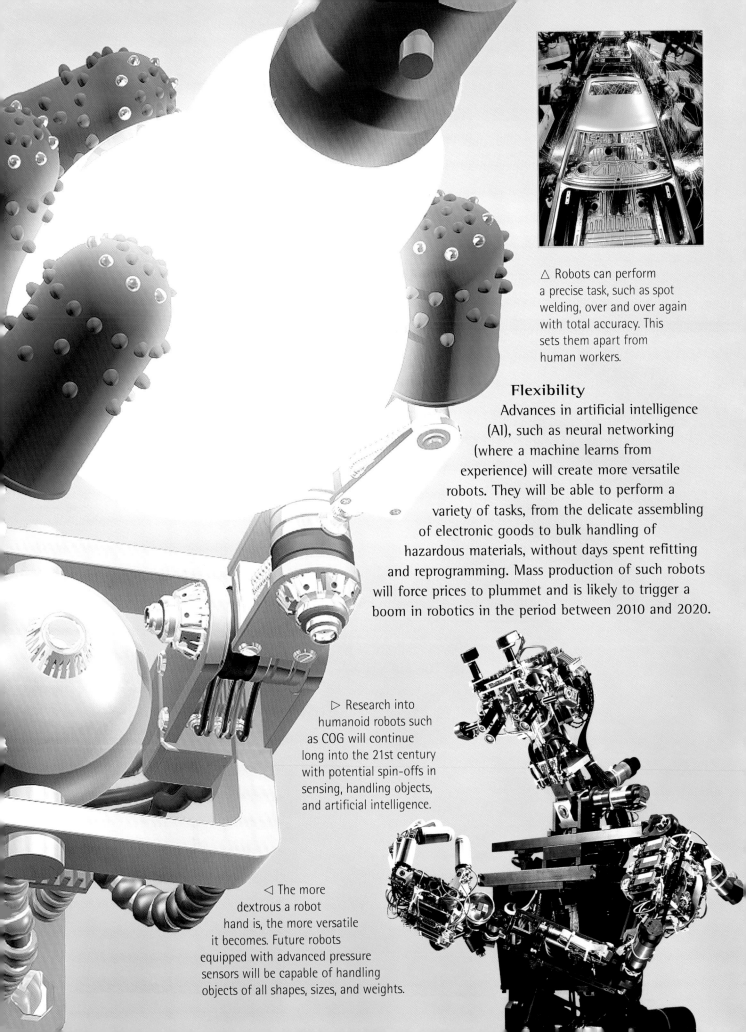

△ Robots can perform a precise task, such as spot welding, over and over again with total accuracy. This sets them apart from human workers.

Flexibility

Advances in artificial intelligence (AI), such as neural networking (where a machine learns from experience) will create more versatile robots. They will be able to perform a variety of tasks, from the delicate assembling of electronic goods to bulk handling of hazardous materials, without days spent refitting and reprogramming. Mass production of such robots will force prices to plummet and is likely to trigger a boom in robotics in the period between 2010 and 2020.

▷ Research into humanoid robots such as COG will continue long into the 21st century with potential spin-offs in sensing, handling objects, and artificial intelligence.

◁ The more dextrous a robot hand is, the more versatile it becomes. Future robots equipped with advanced pressure sensors will be capable of handling objects of all shapes, sizes, and weights.

SMART FACTORIES

The Industrial Revolution in Europe in the 1700s and 1800s altered the way most people had been working for thousands of years. Time-consuming work by individuals was replaced by factories that grouped together large numbers of people and machinery. During the 20th century, assembly lines, automation, and early industrial robots increased productivity and made it possible to manufacture great numbers of affordable products. The smart factory of the 21st century will make products even more easily available and cheaper to buy. Smart factories will depend on advances in artificial intelligence, robotics, and automation processes to create factories that can function with almost no human involvement.

△ Working conditions in factories of the 1800s were often dirty, cramped, and dangerous. People were forced to perform boring, repetitive tasks for hours on end.

▷ Automatic guided vehicles (AGVs) carry materials and parts between automated processes. Here, an AGV ferries a car shell along an assembly line in Turin, Italy.

◁ Completely automated factories will feature self-checking equipment, maintenance robots, and computer networks that constantly check that the factory is running smoothly.

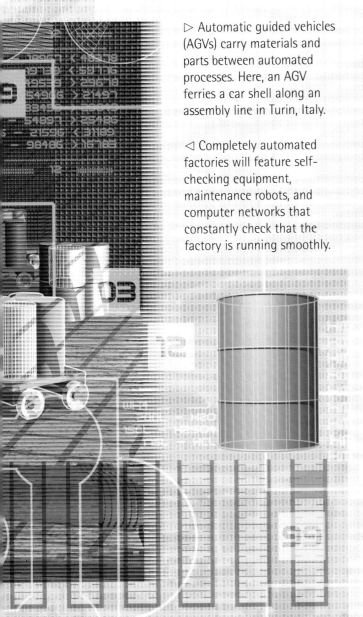

Remote factories

By 2030, smart factories will be able to operate with a minimum of human help. These factories will feature self-checking equipment, robot maintenance and repair, and a mixture of software and robot supervision. Unlike factories of the past, they will not need to be located near large towns, which in earlier times would have provided the workforce. Instead, they may be built in remote sites or near raw material sources.

Consumer power

With competition even more intense than in the previous century, 21st-century manufacturers will offer products made in automated factories, but made to fit each individual customer's needs. Shoppers will be able to choose exactly which options they want from an extensive list of options. The data will be be sent over a computer network to a smart factory that will manufacture and send the product rapidly, whether it is a car or a new pair of shoes.

Self-assembly

Artificial intelligence, as well as more powerful and accurate sensors, are vital keys to developing industrial robots. As robots become easier to use, their cost will drop. By 2025, robots, just like other 21st-century products, will be built in smart factories by other robots.

BLURRED VISION

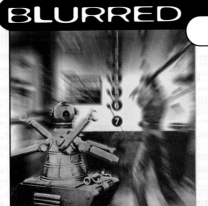

Many people once feared that robots would rebel against their human masters. Instead, robots have become just one of the many automatic features of the advanced factory.

MICROMACHINES

Machines have been getting smaller and smaller for decades. The arrival of electronic components, such as the transistor and integrated circuits, have helped shrink many machines to a fraction of their previous size. But miniaturization is not just about shrinking, it is also about packing more functions into the same size unit. Ballpoint pens, for example, were once used only for writing. Today, some have a clock, radio, and voice recorder built in. The driving forces behind miniaturization have come from the needs of various space programs, the development of new materials, and, most important, advances in computer technology.

△ Valves used in early electronics were often unreliable. The invention of the transistor in 1947 was a giant step toward the development of micromachinery.

MEMs

MicroElectroMechanical systems, or MEMs for short, are complete machines or components built to the same miniature scale as the circuitry on a silicon chip. Devices—from motors and sensing systems the size of a pollen grain to pumps the size of a pinhead—could transform engineering in the same way that the silicon chip led to the computer revolution.

▽ Swarms of tiny, cheaply manufactured robot helicopters may be with us by the 2020s. These machines could monitor the condition of crops and get rid of harmful insect pests, without mass spraying of insecticides.

◁ Microengineering has produced many scaled-down devices, including this working race car less than an inch (25mm) long. The motor powering the car is about $\frac{1}{10}$ of an inch (2.4mm) in diameter.

Office on an arm

The building blocks are already in place to make portable offices worn as a gauntlet, bracelet, or head-set. Processing and memory components are already small enough to be held in the palm of the hand. One problem that remains is how human and machine will communicate. Miniature keyboards, for example, are difficult to use. Speech recognition is one solution. One day, direct thought control may be possible, too.

Working together

Breakthroughs in microengineering and robotics will lead to the rise of many-robot systems. These will consist of robots working together side-by-side. These machines will be capable of learning from their collective experience in the same way that bees and termites do. As early as 2010, many-robot systems will be performing a variety of tasks such as minesweeping or land surveying.

△ These micromachine parts are shown next to a fly's leg for scale. Built using techniques similar to the creation of silicon chips, micromotors and machines could be used extensively in industry by 2025.

NANOTECHNOLOGY

Nanotechnology is the ultimate in thinking small when it comes to machines. The term comes from the word nanometer, a measurement of one millionth of a centimeter or the equivalent of about ten atoms long. Nanotechnology is technology and machinery that has been created to this scale. The impact of nanotechnology on almost every area of our lives is potentially limitless. Nanomachines could work within other machines and other objects, maintaining them so that they never break down or wear out. Self-repairing car engines and clothing will reduce waste and usher in a new age. According to one nanotechnology expert, Ralph Merkle, "Nanotechnology can be the cornerstone of future technology, a fundamental factor in the future development of civilization."

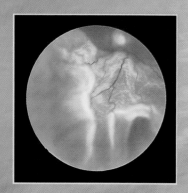

△ A detached retina is an eye condition that can lead to permanent blindness. By 2060, surgery for this condition, as well as many others, will be transformed by nanotechnology.

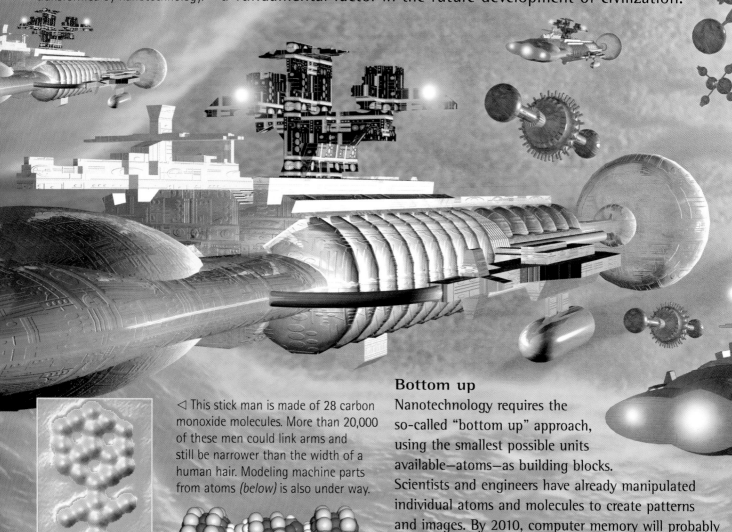

◁ This stick man is made of 28 carbon monoxide molecules. More than 20,000 of these men could link arms and still be narrower than the width of a human hair. Modeling machine parts from atoms (below) is also under way.

Bottom up

Nanotechnology requires the so-called "bottom up" approach, using the smallest possible units available—atoms—as building blocks. Scientists and engineers have already manipulated individual atoms and molecules to create patterns and images. By 2010, computer memory will probably use nanotechnology to store vast amounts of data on tiny clusters of atoms and molecules. By 2020, we can expect the first nanomachines to be made.

Saving the planet

Nanotechnology could create paint for road markings full of very small solar cells that generate pollution-free electricity from solar power. Smart engines could include nanomachines that reduce polluting waste compounds. Fleets of nanorobots, known as nanobots, created in huge numbers, could work to repair the ozone layer or clean up areas of the world polluted by older technology.

Working inside you

One of the most exciting goals of nanotechnology is the creation of nanomachines that can repair our bodies from the inside. This would revolutionize our health. Medical nanobots could enter the bloodstream, scrubbing our blood vessels free of cholesterol and unblocking clogged arteries and veins. Smart toothpaste could contain fleets of nanobots that detect and remove plaque.

△ At present, oil slicks cause major pollution problems. An army of nanobots could work at a microscopic level, breaking down and reprocessing an oil slick before serious damage is done.

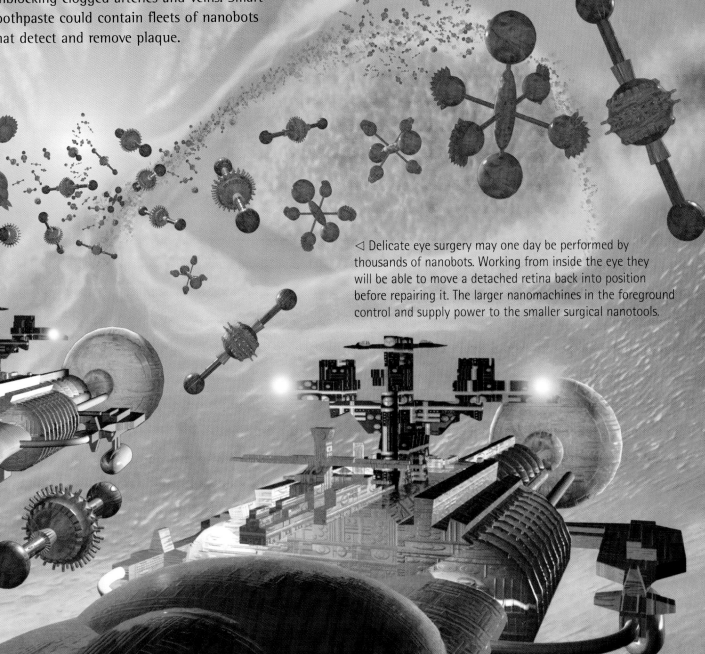

◁ Delicate eye surgery may one day be performed by thousands of nanobots. Working from inside the eye they will be able to move a detached retina back into position before repairing it. The larger nanomachines in the foreground control and supply power to the smaller surgical nanotools.

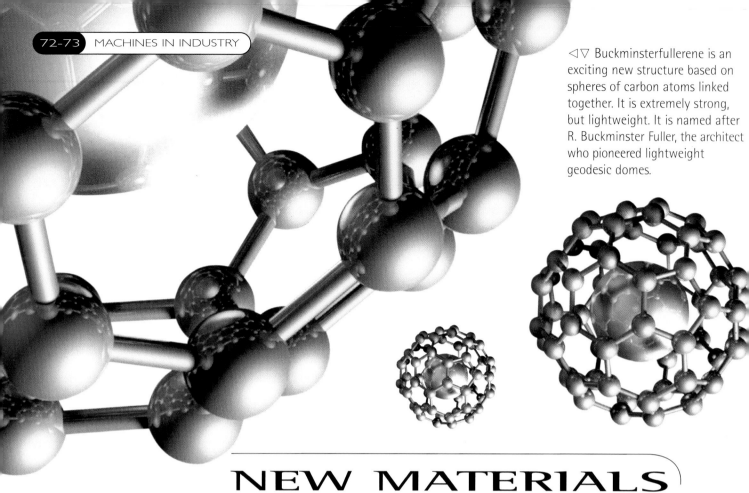

◁▽ Buckminsterfullerene is an exciting new structure based on spheres of carbon atoms linked together. It is extremely strong, but lightweight. It is named after R. Buckminster Fuller, the architect who pioneered lightweight geodesic domes.

NEW MATERIALS

Humans have always had the urge to create something new from the raw materials found on earth. From the discovery of metal alloys created by mixing base metals together in the Bronze Age over 4,000 years ago, to the creation of plastics from oil and petroleum, this drive for new materials has helped shape civilization. In the future we can expect to see many new materials, or developments of old ones. Some of these materials will offer improvements in areas such as strength, heat-resistance, and recyclability. Others will offer radically new and unexpected benefits.

△ Nylon stockings appeared in the early 1940s. They were one of the first products to be developed by processing oil.

Composites

Composite materials are made of several different materials bonded together. Since the early 1970s, they have had a huge impact on many machines and products, from personal defense armor to spacecraft. Important composite materials include Kevlar, glass-reinforced plastic (GRP), metal matrix composites, and carbon-reinforced ceramics.

△ Lycra is a fabric that reduces muscle vibration, a major cause of muscle fatigue. This can help athletes perform better.

Shape Memory Alloys (SMAs) can remember their original shape and return to it after being stretched or compressed. By the end of the 21st century, homes, offices, and other structures built with SMA materials will be capable of withstanding earthquakes.

△ At 330x magnification, the individual fibers of fiberglass can be seen clearly. Fiberglass is a strong but lightweight composite material.

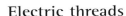

◁ Glasses made with Shape Memory Alloys have already been produced. They do not break—even after being crumpled and crushed.

Electric threads

Smart materials are able to react and adapt to their environment. They are already found in light sensitive sunglasses and "breathable" fabrics. Electrotextiles is one exciting area of development. Researchers have created fibers with carbon in them that can transmit electric signals. Electrotextiles could be used in nerve-stimulating body suits for people with disabilities or in clothes that contain complete communication systems.

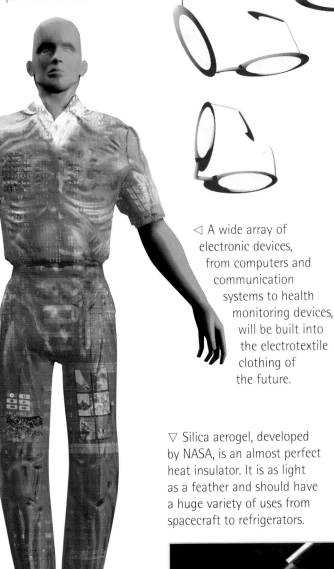

◁ A wide array of electronic devices, from computers and communication systems to health monitoring devices, will be built into the electrotextile clothing of the future.

▽ Silica aerogel, developed by NASA, is an almost perfect heat insulator. It is as light as a feather and should have a huge variety of uses from spacecraft to refrigerators.

New materials, new possiblities

Computers, airliners, and many other 20th-century inventions would not have been possible without plastics, new metal alloys, and silicon. New materials in the 21st century will help drive technology in a similar way. Areas that are likely to benefit from advances in materials include superconductivity, nuclear fusion, and virtual reality.

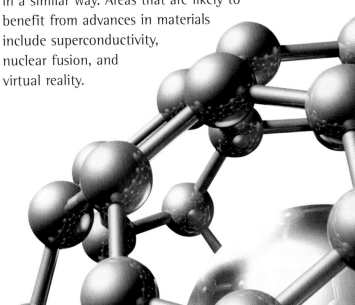

CREATING POWER

Machines have always needed power to work. Until the 1800s, most machines, such as bellows or plows, only required the muscular effort of humans or animals. A few, such as waterwheels, were driven by the channeling of simple, natural movement. The advent of electricity and the internal combustion engine changed machines forever. Today, power generating plants, oil refineries, and petroleum production sites feed the world's insatiable demand for power. During the 20th century, power consumption increased more than ten times. By the year 2020, world demand for power will have increased again by at least 50 percent. Many of the fuels used today will not last forever. This fact, together with growing environmental concerns, will lead to a greater emphasis on efficient power production, storage, and use. Research into potentially vital areas, such as superconductivity, nuclear fusion, and alternative, renewable energies, may lead to a major breakthrough that will help us rely less on traditional fuels for power.

2025
Widespread use of photovoltaic cells

2010
Biomass energy increasingly used

2005
Portable computers powered by kinetic and solar energy

1985
Wave energy power plant in operation

1951
First nuclear reactor

1879
First electric power plant

1870
Internal combustion engine first developed

1832
Mechanical energy converted into electric energy

1800
Electric cell, forerunner of battery, invented

1700s
First practical, working steam engines

c. 400 B.C.
Waterwheel used as source of power in the Middle East

FOSSIL FUELS

Coal, oil, and natural gas power the modern world. Formed over millions of years, these fossil fuels are created by layers of soil and rock, which have compressed decaying animal and plant matter. During the early decades of the 21st century, humans will continue to rely on these fossil fuels, despite the ecological problems created by the air waste gases. Fossil fuels are a finite, nonrenewable resource—they will not last forever at the rate we are using them. Supplies are decreasing, although not as quickly as predicted in the 1960s and 1970s. Since then, new techniques for finding and getting fossil fuels have led to the discovery and recovery of previously unknown supplies.

△ Our great need for coal and oil has resulted in massive mining operations all over the world, such as this open-pit mine in Germany. The demand for fossil fuels will continue for many decades to come.

◁ One alternative to gasoline is biofuel, which is made from processing certain plants. Improvements in this process may lead to much more widespread use of biofuel.

△ Connah's Quay gas-fired power plant, North Wales, U.K. uses an advanced system called combined cycle gas turbine (CCGT) It is 40 percent more efficient than a regular coal-fired station.

Remote operation

Even with advances in solar power and other alternative energies, fossil fuels will still be needed both as a fuel and as a raw material for plastics and other substances. The search for new supplies, from 2015 onward, will be done by a new generation of robots and intelligent machines. By 2030, remote ocean mining and drilling will take place in many parts of the world. Drilling rigs and coal mines will also be operated remotely in areas that are difficult to live in, such as deserts.

Nightmare scenario

The dwindling of fossil fuels will have a major impact on the planet. We are dependent on machines—many of which rely on fossil fuels to make them work. No power means no machines, and society would grind to a halt. Even a major increase in fuel prices could lead to a catastrophic world recession, because the economy is directly linked to the price of fossil fuels. The search for alternative energy sources will become more and more important during the 21st century.

More efficiency

With the world demand for electricity expected to double by 2020, there will be major efforts to make more efficient use of fossil fuels in the 21st century. One way to achieve this is to improve the way we store electricity and transmit it. Maintaining power lines will become vital, and by 2015, we can expect to see special power line robots working more quickly, safely, and efficiently than humans can.

◁ Core samples taken from the arctic wastelands, or tundra, indicate that there are large oil and gas deposits. By 2025, remote automated drilling platforms may be built there. They will require only rare maintenance visits from human personnel.

The search for fuels and other resources may eventually lead to exploration and mining of planets other than the earth. By 2100, mining units might recover ore from the moon and asteroids. The ore will be reprocessed into high-grade fuel and then transported back to earth.

▽△ By 2018, maintenance robots powered by fans and small air thrusters will hover around power lines. Armed with gripping and cutting tools, they will monitor a line's condition and make repairs.

ENERGY FROM ATOMS

△ Calder Hall was the first nuclear power plant in the U.K. It began generating electricity in 1956 and is still in use today.

Nuclear fission—the process of splitting atoms—generates previously unimagined amounts of power without using up fossil fuel supplies. However, nuclear power does have serious disadvantages. The high levels of radioactivity generated pose a potentially lethal health risk. There are also enormous costs involved in safeguarding against such risks and dealing with radioactive waste. Nuclear power development is slow at present, but, if fossil fuel supplies dwindle and global warming fears increase, it is possible that the 21st century will see nuclear power play an important role as a power resource.

Public image

Nuclear power produces few of the polluting gases that cause acid rain or global warming. However, unlike other technologies in the 21st century, nuclear power will have to overcome negative public opinion. Confidence in nuclear power took a sharp downturn after incidents such as the 1986 Chernobyl disaster in the Ukraine, and the continuing concerns over waste disposal. Scientists will continue to work to reduce risks and develop safer nuclear power.

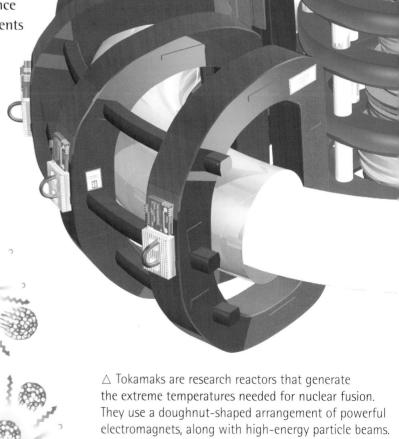

△ Tokamaks are research reactors that generate the extreme temperatures needed for nuclear fusion. They use a doughnut-shaped arrangement of powerful electromagnets, along with high-energy particle beams.

◁ In nuclear fission a neutron collides with an unstable U-235 atom, causing it to split. This releases more neutrons and a great deal of energy. With more U-235 atoms present, this sets off a chain reaction.

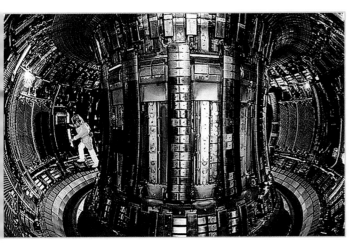

△ This tokamak fusion reactor is part of the Joint European Torus project in the U.K. Other research establishments use lasers to generate the necessary heat.

Waste disposal

The disposal of the high-level radioactive waste created by the nuclear power process is a huge problem. The waste has to be stored for as long as 10,000 years before its radioactivity drops to harmless levels. Most of the world's nuclear waste is in temporary storage facilities awaiting a decision on its fate. By 2010, permanent facilities for long-term storage will have to be built despite the fierce public debate that may arise when it comes to finding a place for them.

▷ Vitrification holds radioactive waste in an inert glass or ceramic compound. It is then encased in a heavy, metal cannister prior to being buried underground.

The holy grail

In the process of nuclear fusion, heavy hydrogen atoms join together to form helium in a self-sustaining reaction that produces enormous amounts of energy. However, this only occurs at temperatures of millions of degrees Fahrenheit. Scientists are developing different ways of heating atoms to these levels and building a container that can safely handle such temperatures. Whether the goal of safe and unlimited commercial nuclear fusion is a possibility is a question that is not likely to be answered until the middle of the 21st century.

△ Fast breeder reactors, like Dounreay in Scotland, can produce up to 60 times the energy of a regular nuclear fission reactor. However, there are still technological problems and high costs.

BLURRED VISION

In the 1930s, nuclear power promised a golden age of cheap, clean, limitless energy. By the mid-1950s, when nuclear power plants were first built, long-term waste storage and fears of contamination were major issues.

ENERGY FROM THE CORES

Nuclear fusion—the process behind the sun's awesome power—has provided the earth with energy for billions of years. However, the fraction of the sun's output that reaches earth is a staggering 30,000 times more than the energy we actually use. This incredible resource will give us sustainable, pollution-free power if scientists can learn how to use it more efficiently. Although it is small in comparison to the sun's energy, the earth's core also generates considerable heat. Work continues on geothermal technologies that will harness some of this heat energy and convert it into electrical power. In the future, it is likely to increase in importance as an additional, pollution-free energy supply.

△ The technology behind solar power is not new. This solar cooker, which boils the water in a coffee pot, dates back to the 1960s.

△ Solar-powered calculators have been available since the 1970s. They use photovoltaic cells to convert sunlight into electrical power.

Solar heat

One form of solar power generation makes use of the sun's warming energy. It uses solar heat reflectors to gather the sun's heat and focus it on a collector. Heat collectors work like radiators in reverse—they collect heat that is used to boil a liquid, such as oil or water. In the case of water, the steam that is created drives electricity-generating turbines.

△ This solar reflector in the Pyrenees in France is made up of 9,500 mirrors and automatically turns to follow the sun.

Sunlight power

Light energy from the sun can also generate solar power. Photovoltaic cells consist of two layers. When the light strikes the top layer of cells, it knocks electrons free from their atoms. These electrons move between the two layers, helping to generate an electric current. As photovoltaic cells become more efficient and cheaper to manufacture, a boom in solar power is likely to occur. In the coming years, photovoltaic cells will appear on cars, buildings, and even clothing, where they could power lightweight electronic devices.

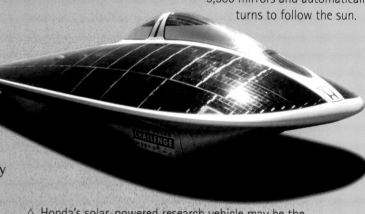

△ Honda's solar-powered research vehicle may be the forerunner of solar vehicles found on the road by the 2020s.

Hot rocks

Geothermal power uses energy from under the earth's surface to heat water. This water is either used to supply heating and hot water to nearby homes and factories, or it is pumped through a heat exchanger. This converts it into steam that is used to drive electricity generators. From 2020 onward, geothermal power plants will become more common as breakthroughs in drilling deeper into the earth and the use of Hot Dry Rock (HDR) technology make it possible to build geothermal plants in many more locations.

△ Icelandic bathers enjoy the hot water generated by a geothermal power plant. These power plants are located in areas of intense thermal activity.

△ Future geothermal power plants may be completely automatic and sited in areas of great thermal, or even volcanic, activity. They will be remote controlled from a distance by human technicians. Maintenance robots and machines will monitor and make routine repairs.

▽ Each panel of this solar power plant consists of thousands of solar cells and a grid of metal conductors that turn sunlight into an electrical current.

HARNESSING THE ELEMENTS

△ The mechanical power created by waterwheels has been used for centuries to grind corn and pump water.

Fears that fossil fuel supplies were running low, and concerns about the damage caused by their emissions, led to much research in the late 20th century on alternative, low-pollution forms of power. Nature provides us with potential energy sources that are endless, even if they are not constant. The movement of wind, waves, and tides can all be turned into useful energy. In the 21st century, scientists and engineers will continue to work on creating efficient, cost-effective energy generation from wind and water. A major breakthrough will make a huge difference in the way future generations obtain power.

△ The first tidal power plant was built in France across the Rance River. It has been in operation since 1966.

Water power

Hydroelectric power (HEP) uses the force of water flowing downward to move turbines that generate electricity. Different types of turbine are used for different geographical locations. The largest current scheme is at Itaipu on the Brazil–Paraguay border, and it generates 10,000 megawatts of power. Research into new, more efficient types of turbines will result in a number of hydroelectric projects across the globe exceeding this power-generating figure by 2015.

▽ Offshore wind farms could be a feature of many coastlines in the future. Denmark is leading the way. By 2030, it is estimated that more than 25 percent of all Denmark's electricity will be generated by offshore wind farms.

△ Mountainous locations and large dams, such as the Hoover Dam in Arizona, provide a fast-flowing water source needed to make a hydroelectric project effective.

Farming the wind

Wind power spins a wind turbine's blades, which cause a generator to turn and create electricity. As materials and low-friction design technologies are developed, wind turbines will increase in efficiency. Located together in large numbers on open land, hilltops, and even offshore, wind farms are likely to become an increasingly important source of efficient energy. Even so, there are still concerns about their environmental impact, because wind farms are noisy and spoil the landscape.

◁ The blades of this experimental Vertical Axis Wind Turbine allow it to work regardless of wind direction.

Waves and tides

Since ancient times, the power of the waves and the tides of the oceans has inspired awe in many people. The prospect of harnessing this power has excited many researchers. However, the major obstacle is the size and cost of structures that stretch across rivers, estuaries, and seas. By the year 2025, even though a number of tidal and wave power plants may be in operation, they are likely to be overshadowed by massive increases in wind and solar power generation.

◁ The first battery was invented in 1800 by the Italian scientist Alessandro Volta and called a voltaic pile. It consisted of disks of copper, zinc, and cardboard saturated with a salt solution.

▽ A technique called computational fluid dynamics (CFD) allows computers to check on the effects of gases and liquids around an object such as this space plane. CFD helps scientists cut down friction and other energy waste.

GREATER EFFICIENCY

Once a machine is invented, people have usually tried to improve its efficiency–to make it do more with less power. This will become even more vital in the future–especially with growing worries about the effects of some kinds of power on the environment. Scientists and engineers are researching new ways of getting more with less by improving design, streamlining, and using advanced materials. Greater efficiency is a goal for all future machines–not just the electronic and mechanical machines and the vehicles that consume power, but also the power plants and transmission devices that generate power in the first place.

◁ A combination of lightweight materials and a streamlined design are behind the incredible performance of this record-breaking race bike.

Electric power

New power plants are able to produce electricity with less fuel than was required in the 20th century. Improved technology will transmit the electricity to homes, offices, and factories more efficiently. Batteries are also likely to improve. The superbatteries of the 2020s will store far more electricity than today's. Many more batteries will be rechargeable and easier to recycle.

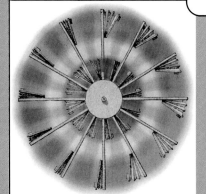

The idea of a perpetual motion machine, which, once you start it, makes enough power to keep itself running forever, has occupied many scientists over the centuries. It is now believed that such a machine goes against the laws of physics.

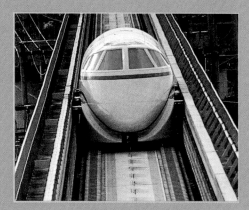

▷ The Japanese Magnetic Levitation (Maglev) train uses powerful electric magnets to raise the train just above the track. The huge reduction in friction results in a faster, more efficient train.

Electricity without energy loss

The ability of certain materials to conduct electricity at incredibly low temperatures with no resistance or power loss is called superconductivity. A lot of research is still needed to develop superconducting materials that are practical to shape and use, and that work at less extreme temperatures. By 2030, we should begin to see superconductors in extremely efficient electric motors and in power lines that can transmit electricity for hundreds of miles without energy loss.

A lack of friction

Friction—the resistance caused by two things rubbing together—creates wear and heat, and reduces the performance of many machines. Research into ways of minimizing friction will continue far into the 21st century. Lubrication systems should improve, computer models will help improve steamlining, and new materials will be created that produce very little friction.

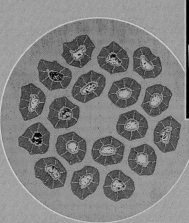

◁△ YBCO is a ceramic superconductor that works at relatively high temperatures. It allows electricity to be conducted without resistance.

2040 Space hotels in operation

2012 Fully automated stores with robot assistants

MACHINES
NEAR AND FAR

Many machines—from the winch used at a water well to weapons such as the cannon—were designed to extend the range of a person's actions. This trend continued throughout the 20th century but with one important advance—machines that could also be operated by remote control were created to be used in dangerous places, such as nuclear power plants. Sophisticated communications and control systems allow teleoperated machines to be controlled by people from a great distance away. Automation is another important development. Automatic machines and robots with basic intelligence are taking over many day-to-day tasks that were once performed by humans. Automated machines are also working far from home, exploring space and the planets in our solar system.

1980s
Domestic robots available

1976
First probe on Mars

1971
Launch of first space
station, Russian *Salyut*

1969
First man on the moon

1957
First satellite in space

1952
Introduction of the credit card

1952
First microwave oven

IN THE HOME

△ The microwave oven, which cuts down the cooking time of many foods, was hailed as the ultimate in labor-saving devices when it was first launched in the 1950s.

During the 20th century, many machines, from washing machines to food processors, were designed to cut down the time spent on household chores. New machines in future homes will work even harder for us. As the cost of microprocessors continues to drop, more and more homes will be controlled by computer networks with a fully programmable series of intelligent electronic functions. These will be built into the house as it is constructed and will include full security systems, climate and environmental control, and advanced telecommunications features.

No cord accord

Wireless power networks will be found in many high-tech homes built after 2015. Most of the electricity required by the network will come from conventional sources, but some will be generated by a home's own solar panels. Many electrical devices, from irons to televisions, will be powered by advanced, superefficient batteries, allowing cordless operation. Electrical outlets will be replaced by recharging stations for these batteries.

Faster food

Advances in food technology and genetic engineering of fresh foods will make washing, cutting, and peeling a thing of the past. Kitchens will eventually be little more than a place where food can be stored, heated, and served. Even so, pots, pans, and chopping boards will not disappear completely. Some people will still prefer to keep the human touch when cooking food.

△ Intelligent kitchens, such as this research model in Seattle, will be standard in homes from 2020. They will feature smart stoves that scan cooking data imprinted on food and apply the correct amount of heat for the right amount of time.

◁ The intelligent garbage can uses magnets and material sensors to sort different types of garbage for recycling.

CRYSTAL BALL

By 2040, conventional carpet cleaning—either by robots or humans—may be a thing of the past. Electronically controlled carpet fibers could move dust and dirt to the edge of the carpet where it would be collected in easy-to-empty containers.

△ By 2020, pans made from smart metal alloys will be able to sense and adjust exactly how much heat they conduct. This will help them prevent, for example, water or sauce from boiling over.

▽▷ Smart glass will be able to measure the amount and intensity of light passing through it and automatically dim the glass if the light is too bright.

Environmental control

Many machines installed in the houses of the future will monitor and adjust different aspects of the environment. Energy conservation will continue to be an important issue. To ensure efficiency, intelligent heating monitors will be found around the house. These will automatically adjust temperatures and be linked to electromechanical devices that open and shut windows and doors in order to reduce the energy used in heating or cooling.

DOMESTIC ROBOTS

It is estimated that by 2015, there will be at least three million robots working in industry. Besides factories, robots will also be used in supermarkets, as security guards, and in hospitals, as carers and helpers. By 2025, office robots and automatic machines will be handling many basic tasks now performed by people, for example, inputting data and handling phone calls. A new generation of home robots will also be developed. Unlike the novelty toy robots of the 1990s, or the one-function machines of 2000–2010, these will be truly versatile robots capable of performing a wide variety of tasks.

△ This robot lawn mower is solar-powered and has simple crash detectors and sensors that keep the mower within its programmed area.

△ Voice-activated toy robots are the starting point for educational robots for young children. Robot teachers will appear in homes from around 2010 onward.

Home help

Some domestic robots are likely to be used as carers for the old, the sick, and the disabled. Robot carers, unlike humans, will not need to take time off for their own lives and will be able to offer 24-hour care and assistance. They will constantly check a home patient's medical condition and send data over a computer network to doctors in a hospital or medical office.

Early learning

Robotic home teachers will provide one-to-one instruction for many young children in the future. Using artificial intelligence, these robots will perform a range of tasks and activities. Robot teachers will help children acquire early learning skills, from basic shape and color recognition to counting, reading, and writing.

▷ The robot assistant of 2030 will have a lightweight robot arm for some physical chores. Most of its work, however, will be done over computer networks. It will communicate directly with these networks using a probe that fits into a special electrical outlet or by using wireless communications systems.

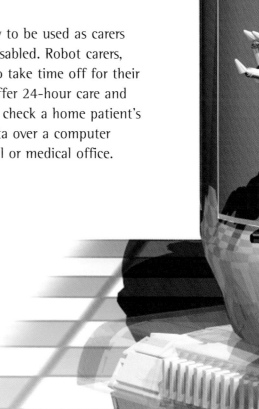

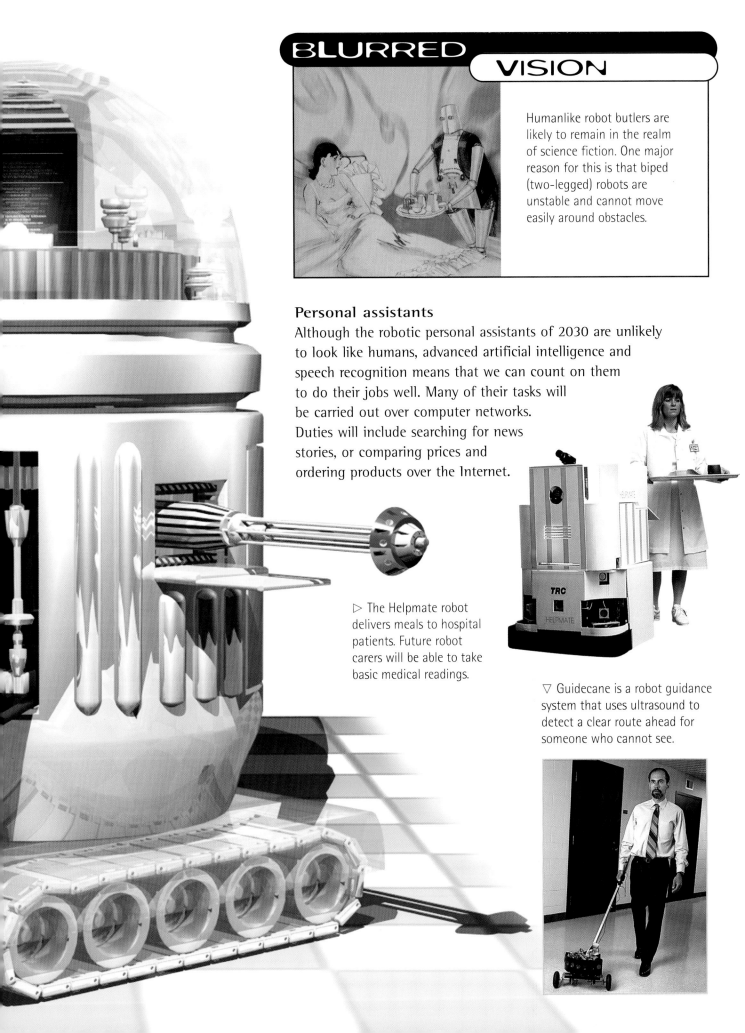

Humanlike robot butlers are likely to remain in the realm of science fiction. One major reason for this is that biped (two-legged) robots are unstable and cannot move easily around obstacles.

Personal assistants

Although the robotic personal assistants of 2030 are unlikely to look like humans, advanced artificial intelligence and speech recognition means that we can count on them to do their jobs well. Many of their tasks will be carried out over computer networks. Duties will include searching for news stories, or comparing prices and ordering products over the Internet.

▷ The Helpmate robot delivers meals to hospital patients. Future robot carers will be able to take basic medical readings.

▽ Guidecane is a robot guidance system that uses ultrasound to detect a clear route ahead for someone who cannot see.

▷ Before computers, banking was slow, time-consuming, and relied on sifting through vast amounts of paper records.

SHOPPING AND BANKING

Shopping, banking, and security will change dramatically during the 21st century. In the late 1990s, many communities had already moved toward electronic currency. Electronic money—in the form of microprocessors that hold a person's complete financial details—will eventually replace paper and coin money. Electronic currency and the growth of the Net for shopping will mean that financial transactions will be handled entirely by machines. This means that machines will need to be able to identify people. Security systems are most likely to be based on biometrics—the scientific measurement of a person's physical features.

Biometrics

Biometrics is expected to become one of the fastest growing industries in the first half of the 21st century. Biometrics uses the unique characteristics of the human voice or a particular part of the body—the face, finger, ear, or eye for example—to identify someone. A biometric system scans one or more of these features and then looks for a match, comparing the information with what is in its memory.

△ Each person's eye has unique features. Sensar is an iris scanning system that creates an eye print and looks for a perfect match in its memory.

Wallet replacement

How will the new electronic currencies be carried? The majority of our credit and financial details will be held in automatic machines that can be accessed using a biometric security system. Microprocessors attached to a smart card, or even implanted within the body, could hold financial records. These devices would also be capable of performing functions such as instant money conversion.

△ At the end of the 1990s, shopping over the Internet was still in its early stages. With improved security and virtual reality (VR) systems, shopping from home or local VR stations is expected to flourish by 2010.

△ This robot shopping cart uses ultrasound to follow a customer around the world's first automated department store, Seibu, in Japan.

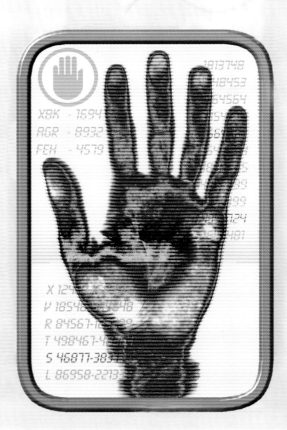

△ Electronic hand scanners could be in use in many countries by 2010.

◁ A user's eye is scanned by an automatic teller machine (ATM) of 2015. The machine may also check other aspects of your face, or scan your hand, before you are allowed to get money or account information.

Watching you

Like it or not, in the 21st century our lives may be constantly watched and many of our actions recorded. It will be possible to track a person's actions through their use of the Internet, credit cards, and smart cards. People will be watched more and more by advanced digital camera systems and closed circuit TV (CCTV). It is likely that the public will campaign to reduce the amount of intrusion into people's lives.

MACHINES IN HAZARDOUS AREAS

Machines are the perfect tools for getting dangerous jobs done or for doing work in hazardous places. Machines have traveled to distant and hostile planets and deep into the depths of the ocean where no human explorers could survive. On land, machines perform jobs that we cannot do in places that we cannot go. Such no-go areas include sites where toxic chemicals and radioactivity are present, the insides of storage tanks and pipelines, in and around volcanoes, or near fierce fires where the heat is intense. As the 21st century progresses, increasingly sophisticated hazard robots, or hazbots, will be developed from materials that are resistant to heat, shock, and other dangers.

△ A bomb disposal robot approaches a bomb. It has a long-reaching robot arm with various tools attached for defusing bombs and controlling explosions.

Defusing the situation

One result of previous military conflicts is that unexploded mines, bombs, and shells (together known as ordnance) are littered all over the world. With a rise in terrorism predicted, bomb disposal robots will be called upon more and more for fast, safe defusing and disposal of unexploded ordnance. Many of these specialized robots will be teleoperated by a human controller positioned at a safe distance.

▷ Future fire-fighting robots will use visual signals and sounds to lead people to escape exits. They will also provide oxygen masks and spray water and other flame-extinguishing substances to cut a safe path through the fire.

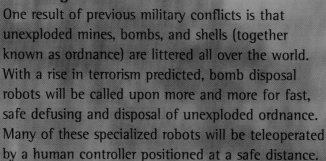

◁ Remote-controlled robot arms are common in the nuclear industry. A person uses hand controls to move the robot's arms. The robot, which is not affected by radiation, can make very precise movements.

Nuclear sites

Radioactivity is a threat to all living things. Machines made of inorganic metals and composites can handle high levels of radioactivity without being damaged, and they are widely used in the nuclear industry. In the future, there will be a growing number of nuclear sites that will have to be taken down and made safe. Automated machines and robots will be essential in this process, known as decommissioning.

Fire-fighting robots

Despite the safeguards that will be built into future buildings, the risk of fire will always exist. Even sophisticated sprinkler systems may not work against a major blaze. By 2020, the use of fire-fighting robots will be standard practice in many places. These will use a range of heat sensors and an internal map of the building to find a way into the heart of the fire area. Once there, the robots will put out the fire with foams and other substances.

△ *Robug 3* is a robot that has the ability to scale walls and ceilings. It uses powerful suckers driven by compressed air to create a partial vacuum under each of its eight feet.

▽ *Dante* is an eight-legged robot designed to move over dangerous, unstable ground. It has successfully made its way into the mouth of Mt. Spurr, an Alaskan volcano.

UNDERWATER MACHINES

Over 70 percent of our planet is covered by water. Our seas and oceans not only contain marine life, but also a huge supply of valuable minerals. As land-based resources become overstretched or exhausted, we will venture under water more and more in search of new supplies. We will also explore the oceans to keep an eye on their ecosystems. Much of this work will be performed by unmanned intelligent machines called Autonomous Underwater Vehicles, or AUVs.

△ Early diving equipment, such as the Klingart diving suit from the late 1700s, only worked at shallow depths.

△ A modern deep-sea diving apparatus encloses the diver in an ultratough shell, pressure-resistant to depths of 220 feet (600m).

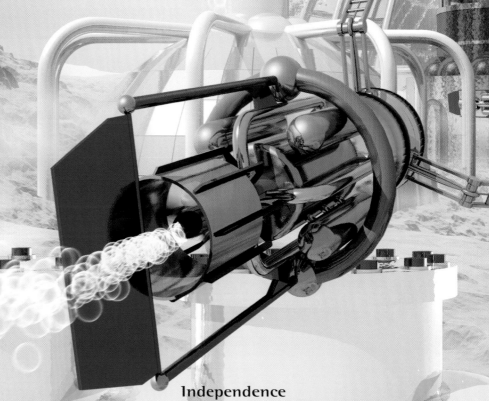

Machine advantages

One of the major problems faced by people exploring under water is that the deeper you go, the greater the water pressure—the pressure doubles every 30 feet (10m) you go down. It is far easier to make unmanned machines that are capable of withstanding the immense pressures found at great depths. Unmanned machines are cheaper to build than manned machines, more maneuverable, and involve no risk to human life.

Independence

At present, Remote Operated Vehicles (ROVs) are controlled by a human operator on the surface and linked by a long cable called a tether. In the future, however, AUVs are likely to take over their role. Using complex sensor and control systems, these machines will operate without direct human control. By 2010, AUVs will be mapping the seabed, as well as maintaining underwater cables and pipelines.

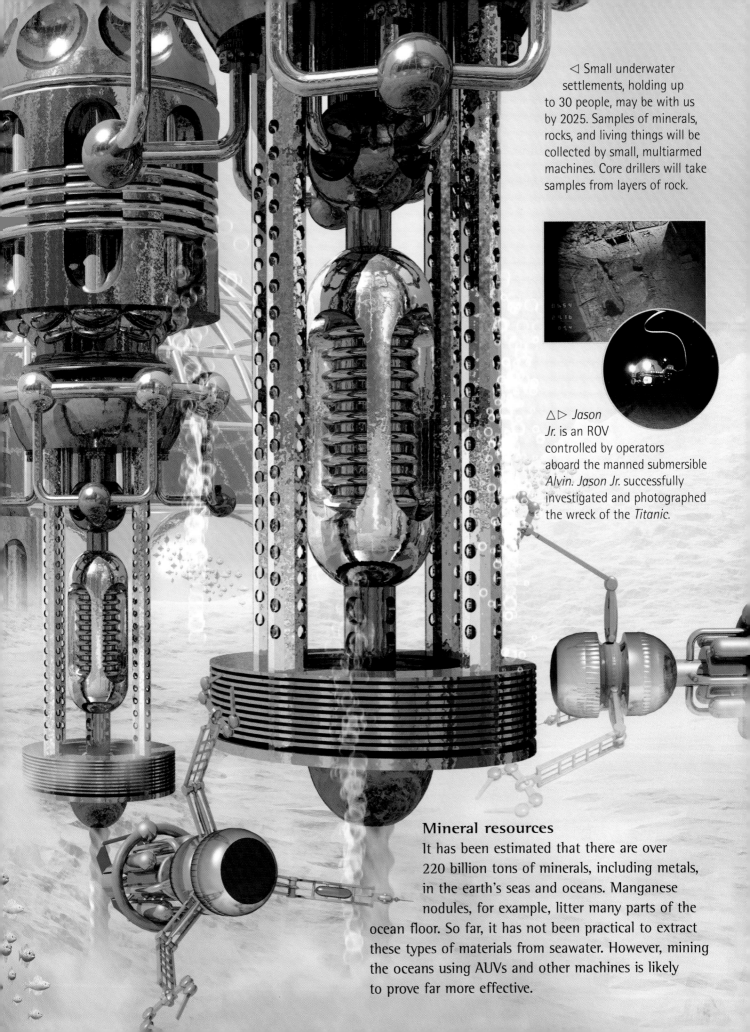

◁ Small underwater settlements, holding up to 30 people, may be with us by 2025. Samples of minerals, rocks, and living things will be collected by small, multiarmed machines. Core drillers will take samples from layers of rock.

△▷ *Jason Jr.* is an ROV controlled by operators aboard the manned submersible *Alvin. Jason Jr.* successfully investigated and photographed the wreck of the *Titanic*.

Mineral resources

It has been estimated that there are over 220 billion tons of minerals, including metals, in the earth's seas and oceans. Manganese nodules, for example, litter many parts of the ocean floor. So far, it has not been practical to extract these types of materials from seawater. However, mining the oceans using AUVs and other machines is likely to prove far more effective.

Man vs. Machine?

Manned spacecraft allow firsthand human experience of space to be recorded, such as the effects of zero gravity on the human body and mind. However, there is no air, water, or food in space. It all has to be carried, along with living quarters for the astronauts. Spacecraft that can support life are more expensive and complex to build than unmanned probes, so a mixture of manned and unmanned missions is likely to continue long into the future.

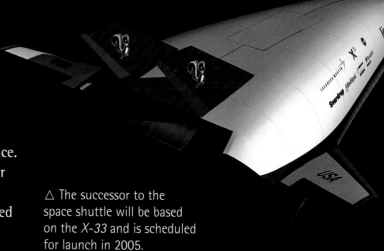

△ The successor to the space shuttle will be based on the *X-33* and is scheduled for launch in 2005.

MACHINES IN SPACE 1

Without machines we would never have been able to leave the earth and explore space. At first, unmanned space probes, launched by rockets, orbited the planet. Astronauts soon followed. These human pioneers relied on the most advanced machinery and technology of their time to keep them alive and get them home safely. Machines paved the way for further manned exploration, first to the moon, in preparation for the manned landings between 1969 and 1972, and then out into the solar system. A number of probes are currently traveling to the far reaches of the solar system and beyond.

△ The *Atlas–Mercury* rocket launched the United States' first manned spaceflight in 1962. Astronaut John Glenn orbited the earth three times.

One-way ticket

Many unmanned machines have been sent into space with zero expectation of their recovery. Probes have been sent near the sun or onto hostile planet surfaces such as Mercury and Venus. Others have journeyed right through the solar system and out into deep space. Experiments and sensors on board the probes are designed to run automatically, sending back data via high-frequency radio waves.

◁ Launched in 1977, *Voyager 1* is now the most distant space probe, 6.5 billion miles away from the earth. Radio signals sent by *Voyager* take almost 10 hours to reach the earth.

△ In November 2004, the *Huygens* probe will be dropped from the *Cassini* orbiter into the atmosphere of Titan, Saturn's largest moon.

◁ The *Apollo 11* mission in 1969 was the first to land men on the moon. They performed a range of experiments there

The moon revisited

Scientific breakthroughs from the International Space Station (ISS) may spark renewed interest in the moon and the establishment of a permanent research colony there. Plans for a lunar observatory on the far side of the moon and a manned mission to Mars may provide the scientific motivation for building the colony. Huge multinational companies that might be interested in the rare minerals found on the moon may provide the sponsorship needed to make the colony a reality.

CRYSTAL BALL

Space launches by 2100 may use incredibly high-powered lasers to heat the air below a craft to temperatures as high as 54,000°F (30,000°C). The thrust generated could be enough to propel the craft into orbit without rockets.

△ A permanent lunar base could be up and running before 2020. It will be constructed with the help of robots and is likely to be nuclear- or solar-powered.

MACHINES IN SPACE 2

Huge amounts of money, time, and effort are needed to send machines and people into space. The International Space Station (ISS), launched in 1998, marks a new age of joint international effort that is likely to kickstart a boom in space technology. Lessons learned from its design, construction, and operation will provide the basis for developing bigger and better space stations. The ISS and future stations will greatly increase our understanding of space science— especially the effects of microgravity, or weightlessness. This is likely to lead to the development of new materials and industrial processes.

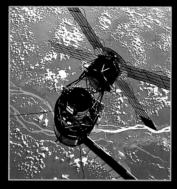

△ *Skylab*, launched in 1973, was the U.S.'s first space station. It proved that humans could live and work in space for extended periods.

△ The Russian *Mir* space station, launched in 1986, is highly automated. Only 13 percent of its operations are done by human beings.

Stepping stone

The ISS is a joint project between 15 different countries, including the United States, Canada, Russia, Japan, and Britain. At least 45 missions will be involved in constructing the most ambitous man-made structure ever built in space. Powered by huge panels of solar cells and equipped with six laboratories, the ISS will provide more than a decade of active service after it is completed in 2004.

△ Working in space involves a combination of machines and astronauts equipped for extravehicular activity (EVA). Here, a satellite capturing device is attached to the end of a space shuttle's robot arm.

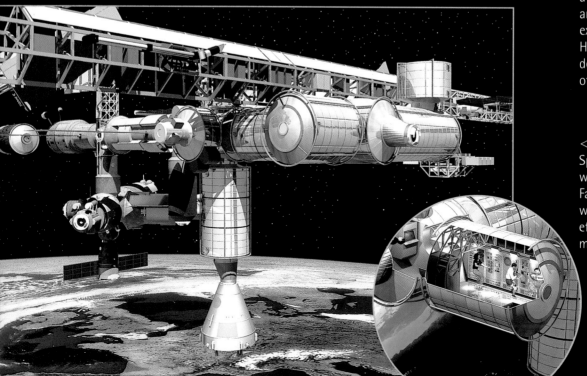

◁▽ One of the International Space Station's many features will be the Columbus Orbital Facility. This pressurized module will be used to study the effects of microgravity on materials and living matter.

▷ Rotating space hotels, shaped like bicycle wheels, may orbit earth by 2040. The spinning motion will create artificial gravity in the outer wheel of the hotel.

All hands on deck

Building any structure in space creates unique problems. Components must be taken into space aboard shuttles and modules launched by rockets. Once in space, astronauts and robots need to work together. Teleoperated robot cameras travel around the site, providing all-over views, while robot grippers move parts into place. Future constructions will be assembled by robots working autonomously– without human help.

Alternative destination

The space program of the 1960s and 1970s led to many unexpected advances in mechanics, robotics, medicine, and computer development. Experiments that take place on future space stations are likely to lead to new areas of scientific research. Space stations could also be used as factories to manufacture new materials or, one day, as vacation spots for space tourists.

OUR NEW HOME

△ *Viking I* was the very first manufactured object to land on the surface of another planet. It reached Mars in 1975 and took soil samples and pictures that were relayed back to mission control on earth.

△In 1997, the *Sojourner* robot, carried by the *Pathfinder* probe, landed on Mars. *Sojourner* was instructed by radio signals sent from the earth, but it also used its own sensors to find a route to a specified target area.

Much of the human race's drive into space has been to learn about the planets and moons that are the earth's neighbors. From the *Apollo* moon landings to probes such as *Voyager* and *Mariner*, sent on flyby trajectories near the major planets, machines have been central to the exploration of other worlds. The planetary rovers and probes of the 1990s were mostly controlled by high frequency radio wave signals sent from mission control on earth. Machines sent out to other planets after 2010 will be highly intelligent and able to act independently, using information gathered by an array of sensors. The information that machines send back to the earth will pave the way for manned missions to Mars from 2025 onward with the hope that, one day, we will be able to live on the planet.

Biospheres

Closed ecology units, sometimes known as biospheres, may be sent to Mars first. These would be constructed by machines and robots before astronauts arrive to live inside them. The units would be closed off from the Martian environment, only taking in solar energy from outside. All wastes would be recycled, and oxygen would be generated using plants grown inside the unit.

A suitable planet

Terraforming is the most ambitious of all future plans for settling on other planets. Terraforming means changing the entire environment of a planet and its atmosphere so that earth plants and animals can live there. Mars, with its low atmospheric pressure and polar ice caps, is the most promising planet for terraforming.

Temperature rising

Mars needs to be warmed up and to have a thicker atmosphere created if the planet is to be terraformed. To achieve this, gases could be pumped into the Martian atmosphere to create a greenhouse effect that would trap more of the sun's heat. If frost and part of the polar ice caps can be melted, they will provide both water on the ground and water vapor in the atmosphere. Genetically engineered bacteria and microbes that absorb carbon dioxide and give out oxygen could be introduced. Although terraforming is a process that takes many thousands of years, we should not underestimate what the future will bring.

△ Closed ecology units, such as the two-acre *Biosphere 2* in Arizona, have already been successfully built on earth.

△ Thousands of years from now, terraforming might transform Mars, creating water reserves and a breathable atmosphere. Lightweight structures could take advantage of the low gravity, while unmanned machines could carry materials and perform maintenance work.

1999
Petronas Towers,
world's tallest
building, completed
in Malaysia

1970s
Use of composite
materials

1934
Fluorescent light
invented

1931
Empire State
Building completed

1892
Reinforced
concrete invented

1885
First skyscraper
built in Chicago

1779
Completion of first
all-metal bridge in
England

3500 B.C.
First cities appear in
Mesopotamia
(now Iraq)

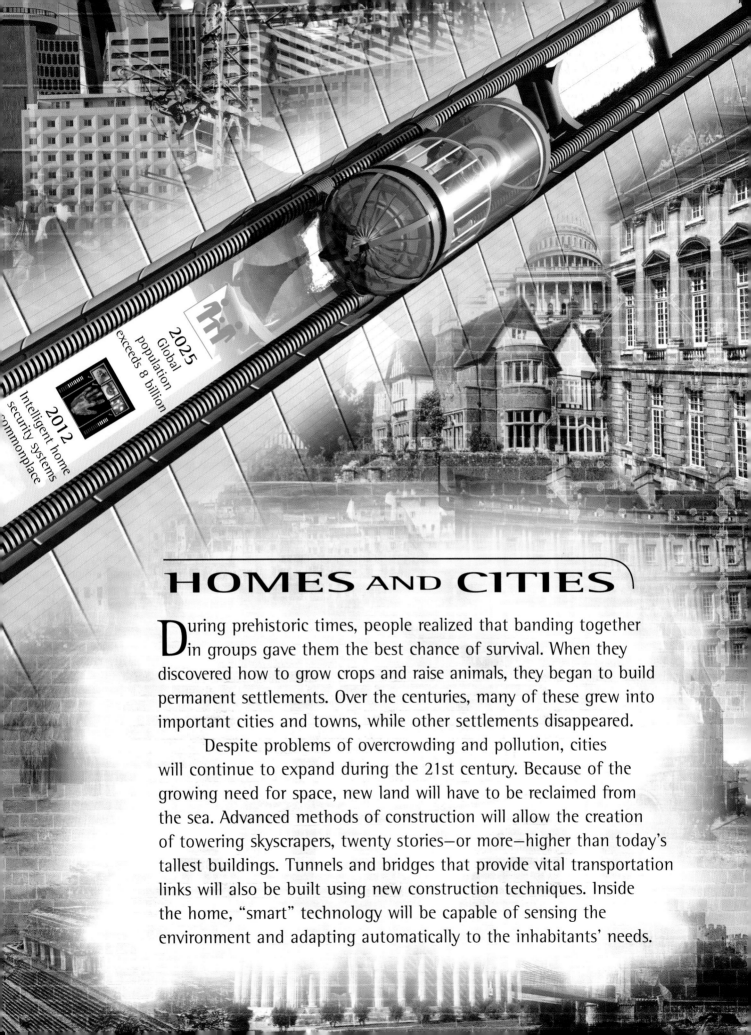

2025
Global
population
exceeds 8 billion

2012
Intelligent home
security systems
commonplace

HOMES AND CITIES

During prehistoric times, people realized that banding together in groups gave them the best chance of survival. When they discovered how to grow crops and raise animals, they began to build permanent settlements. Over the centuries, many of these grew into important cities and towns, while other settlements disappeared.

Despite problems of overcrowding and pollution, cities will continue to expand during the 21st century. Because of the growing need for space, new land will have to be reclaimed from the sea. Advanced methods of construction will allow the creation of towering skyscrapers, twenty stories—or more—higher than today's tallest buildings. Tunnels and bridges that provide vital transportation links will also be built using new construction techniques. Inside the home, "smart" technology will be capable of sensing the environment and adapting automatically to the inhabitants' needs.

FUTURE CITY

Since the development of the first large settlements over 5,000 years ago, people have been living and working in cities and towns. Two hundred years ago, only 2.5 percent of the world's population lived in urban areas. By 2005, over half of the world's population will live in cities, and this figure is expected to keep growing until at least the mid-21st century. The attraction of the city as a seat of power, work, learning, and recreation will continue despite the potential problems created by overcrowding, pollution, and the demands of a growing population.

△ Athens, the capital of Greece, was the most powerful city in the world 2,500 years ago. Its public buildings have inspired architects and builders ever since.

△ Some cities evolve over many centuries. Others, such as Los Angeles, have expanded over a shorter period. In 1890, Los Angeles had a population of 50,000. Today, over nine million people live there.

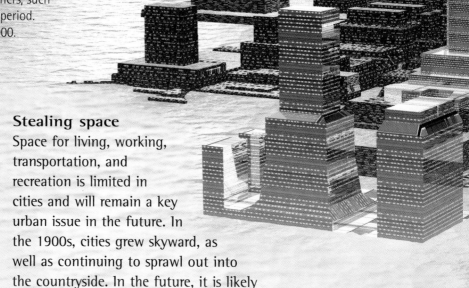

△ As cities grow, they tend to spread out, as shown in this satellite picture of London, England. Towns and villages once outside the city are swallowed up and become part of the urban sprawl.

Stealing space

Space for living, working, transportation, and recreation is limited in cities and will remain a key urban issue in the future. In the 1900s, cities grew skyward, as well as continuing to sprawl out into the countryside. In the future, it is likely that city planners will create space underground for living and working.

Out to sea

Projects to reclaim land from swamps, marshes, and oceans will flourish in wealthy but small nations as a way of increasing available space. There is also the possibility of separate, floating cities; or hybrid, part-floating, part-landbound settlements, linked to the mainland. One proposed scheme is designed to provide living and working space for a million people in a huge, pyramid-shaped structure on the sea off Tokyo, Japan.

▽ As future cities expand, they will make use of all available space, including water if possible. Environmentally-friendly forms of transportation, like airships, will ferry people around this 2030 metropolis.

◁ Air pollution is a major problem that many cities face. Smog created by factories, power plants, and automobile traffic can cause health problems.

Cyber city

Cyberjaya, a city being built in Malaysia, may provide a model for 21st-century cities. In Cyberjaya, gas-fueled vehicles will be banned, low population density—less crowded living—will be encouraged, and every home will be powered by solar energy and connected to the City Command Center—a computer network that provides automated services.

◁ During the English Industrial Revolution in the 1700s and 1800s, many people lived in run-down housing, or slums, when they moved from the countryside to the city.

LIVING TOGETHER

With huge improvements in health care and breakthroughs in the fight against disease, the population of planet earth is booming. It is estimated that by 2025 there will be eight billion people; the number could rise to nine billion in only ten more years. This fast-growing population will place an enormous strain on cities, many of which already suffer from overcrowding and other associated problems. Concerns about traffic control, pollution, and the psychological problems resulting from people living very close together will continue for many years to come.

Social problems

Crowding people together in housing units or skyscrapers is not the best solution to the problem of finding homes for people. In the past, this kind of high-density living has led to major social problems, such as drug abuse and violent crime. The search for more humane ways of housing greater numbers of people will become an important issue in many future cities.

▷ Not all traffic jams are caused by cars. Bicycle rickshaws have created this gridlock in Dhaka, Bangladesh. Unlike cars, however, they are nonpolluting.

◁ This capsule hotel in Tokyo, Japan makes maximum use of the limited living space in the city. Hotel guests sleep in tiny units that are stacked on top of each other.

Designs for living

In existing cities, run-down areas will be redeveloped to house the growing population. In some cases, high-density living and working space will be crammed into a small area. Mass-transit systems and moving walkways will ferry people around. Other areas may choose a low-density, community-led approach with smaller buildings, parks, and car-free zones.

▷ Hong Kong, China, is one of the world's most crowded places. With limited affordable housing, slums are usually the only alternative.

◁ Enclosed walkways at different levels will form an extensive network, connecting many parts of the city. People will be able to move around without having to negotiate the congested streets.

Getting away from it all

From 2010, it is likely that an increasing number of people will turn their backs on city living. Many will move to small cities and towns to escape pollution, congestion, and other urban problems. Advanced communications technology will enable them to telecommute—work from home. Others may go further and opt out of the "rat race" altogether, living in self-sustaining communities in isolated areas.

BLURRED VISION

This imaginary flying city from a 1920s science fiction magazine is one unlikely solution to overcrowding on the planet. Writers and artists have imagined airborne cities since the 1700s.

FUTURE HOMES

In the future, new houses will be designed to cocoon their inhabitants in a secure, comfortable, and highly adaptable environment. Architects, engineers, and designers will draw on important advances in material technology and electronics to create flexible living spaces that can be altered easily by the occupants. Intelligent devices will play an important role in many households. Robot cleaners and smart exercise machines that monitor people's health will be as common as today's microwave ovens and washing machines.

△ Before the 1800s, not many homes had luxuries or comforts. Until labor-saving devices like vacuum cleaners and washing machines appeared in the 1900s, all housework had to be done by hand, and it usually took a long time.

◁ Architects and engineers are rethinking how a house functions both inside and out. This house in California is earthquake resistant and incorporates the latest in energy-saving technology.

Intelligent home

Experts predict that by 2025 the average home will have as much computing power as a nuclear power plant from the 1990s. Computers will be so small and cheap that they will be embedded, or integrated, in almost all our surroundings, from floors to fridges. They will sense our presence and automatically adjust the environment—including light, temperature, and humidity levels—according to our needs.

Flexible living

Formal divisions between rooms are likely to disappear. They will be replaced by a single living space that can be sectioned off with lightweight, but soundproof, movable walls. Multipurpose furniture will occupy living areas. Furniture structure and coverings will change color, shape, and even texture at the user's request. New materials will allow a soft bench seat to transform itself into a table or desk, for example.

▽ The home of 2015 will include furniture that can change its shape and color and walls that serve as giant display screens for information, recreation, or simply to create a relaxing environment. A robot vacuum cleaner will automatically detect and clean up spills.

▷ Alternative forms of energy, such as wind and solar power, will provide all the energy requirements for an increasing number of homes in the future.

▽ Keys will be replaced by biometric systems that scan a person's features before allowing access (below right).

Safe and secure

Traditional locks and keys will be replaced by security systems that scan a person's hand, eye, or face and use biometrics to determine who can enter. Arrays of closed circuit TV (CCTV) cameras will be linked to a network of home security sensors far more sophisticated than today's burglar alarms. If an unauthorized person tries to enter, the house will lock up like a clam and automatically notify the police. It may even use gas sprays or hoses that "fire" harmless sticky foam to prevent the intruder from escaping.

△ Some architects and builders are rejecting the latest technology in favor of simple homes constructed from natural, locally-sourced materials.

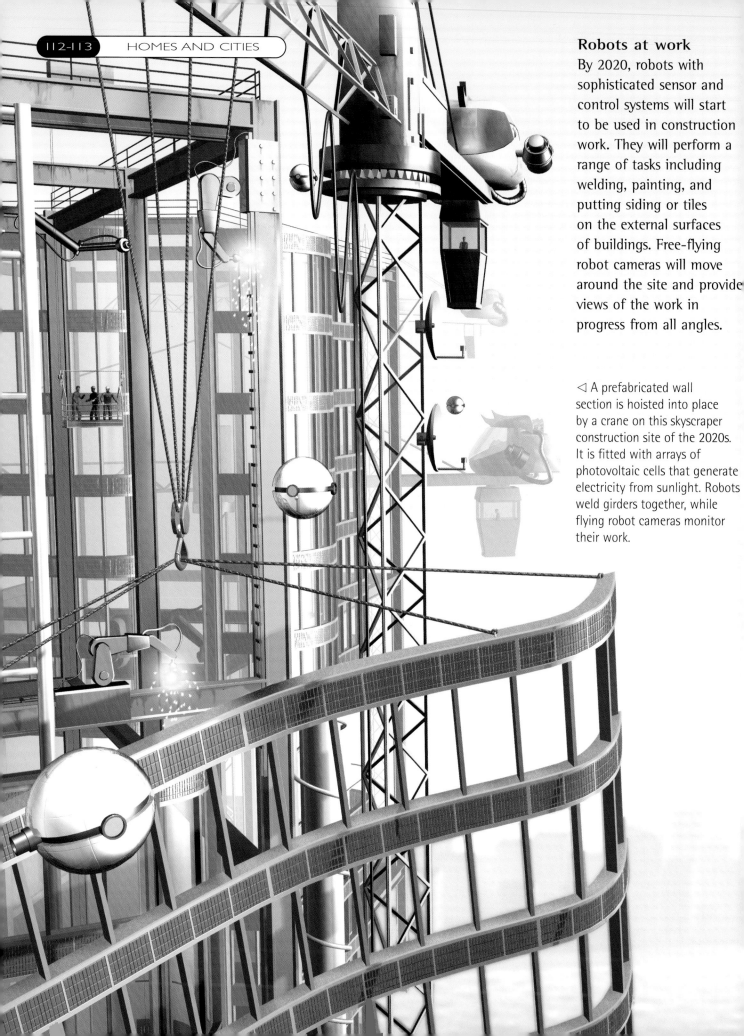

Robots at work

By 2020, robots with sophisticated sensor and control systems will start to be used in construction work. They will perform a range of tasks including welding, painting, and putting siding or tiles on the external surfaces of buildings. Free-flying robot cameras will move around the site and provide views of the work in progress from all angles.

◁ A prefabricated wall section is hoisted into place by a crane on this skyscraper construction site of the 2020s. It is fitted with arrays of photovoltaic cells that generate electricity from sunlight. Robots weld girders together, while flying robot cameras monitor their work.

◁ Construction of the Empire State Building began in March 1930 and was completed in May 1931. It has 102 stories and contains over 178 miles (285km) of steel beams.

Hazard proof

Earthquakes pose a serious threat to some of the world's major cities including San Francisco and Tokyo, Japan. New construction techniques are helping to make some structures more earthquake resistant. The Tokyo Forum building, for example, has glass walls supported independently of the roof. During an earthquake, the roof rocks on powerful joints, preventing the building from crashing down.

CONSTRUCTION

Materials are at the very heart of the construction industry. In the foreseeable future, buildings will continue to be built using steel, concrete, bricks, and glass, but composite materials and metal alloys will also be used. These new materials, along with advanced computer modeling, will allow architects and engineers to design even bigger buildings, tunnels, and bridges and to construct them in places that are currently considered unsuitable. A further innovation will be tiny sensors inside the materials that automatically measure and report any deterioration.

△ Geodesic domes are strong, lightweight structures that do not require internal supports. They are able to enclose large areas using less material than standard frames.

Bridging the gap

Some of the most important construction projects are bridges. The development of exceptionally strong materials, along with computer modeling, is allowing engineers to design increasingly ambitious structures. Proposed projects include the 2-mile (3.3-km) -long Messina Straits Bridge to link mainland Italy and Sicily, and a 3-mile (5-km) -long bridge across the Straits of Gibraltar to join Europe and North Africa.

◁ Powerful computers allow engineers to test structures for stresses and strains long before they are built.

▷ The 1,506 ft. (451m) high Petronas Towers in Malaysia have over 32,000 windows.

CRYSTAL BALL

An increasing number of homes will be built underground during the 21st century. Underground homes offer a spacious alternative to cramped conditions on the surface and are naturally cool, even in very hot climates.

TRANSPORTATION

Until the middle of the 1800s, most people rarely traveled more than a few miles from their homes. When they set out on a journey, their travel choices were limited—boat, ship, horse, or foot. With the invention of the steam locomotive in the 1800s and, later, the development of road vehicles and aircraft, modern transportation opened up a whole new world for many people. During the 21st century, many forms of transportation will become faster, safer, and less harmful to the environment. Electric-powered cars, which cause minimal pollution, will be commonplace on the roads by 2025. Shipping and railroads will also benefit from exciting new forms of power, such as magnetic propulsion. For longer journeys, hypersonic and suborbital airliners could cut flying time by up to two thirds.

1908
First mass-produced car, the Model T Ford

1903
First flight made by a heavier-than-air craft, the Wright brother's Flyer

1830
Intercity railroad service is introduced between Manchester and Liverpool, England

1790
The velocipede, forerunner of the modern bicycle, is invented

1640
The first taxi service begins in Paris

1959
First commercial hovercraft service in operation

1981
French TGV high-speed train service introduced

2010
New generation of safe airships carries passengers and heavy goods

2035
It takes under two hours to fly halfway around the world

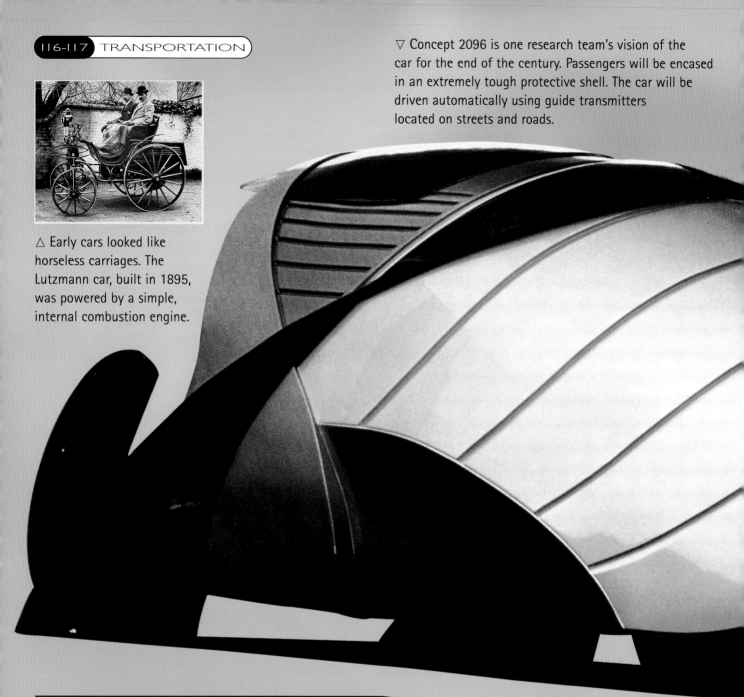

▽ Concept 2096 is one research team's vision of the car for the end of the century. Passengers will be encased in an extremely tough protective shell. The car will be driven automatically using guide transmitters located on streets and roads.

△ Early cars looked like horseless carriages. The Lutzmann car, built in 1895, was powered by a simple, internal combustion engine.

FUTURE CARS

When the first cars took to the roads in the 1880s and 1890s, their top speed rarely exceeded 12 mph (20km/h). The brakes were usually ineffective, and engines often exploded. A century ago, no one could have predicted the global increase in road vehicles, which today number hundreds of millions. Modern cars may be faster, more comfortable, and more fuel-efficient than their predecessors, but, like the first cars, they rely mostly on pollution-causing oil derivatives. The future is likely to see popular alternatives to purely gasoline-powered vehicles—machines that offer comparable performance, but at a lower cost to the planet.

△ Most of today's electric cars have a limited range and can only travel about 60 miles (100km) before their batteries need to be recharged. This recharging point is built into a parking space in Los Angeles.

Fighting pollution

Although modern internal combustion engine cars are "cleaner" than in the past, their exhaust emissions still cause damage to the atmosphere. Many suggestions have been made about how to decrease the impact. These include more fuel-efficient and lightweight cars and an increase in electric vehicle production. Other initiatives include the promotion of public transportation and the banning of cars from urban centers.

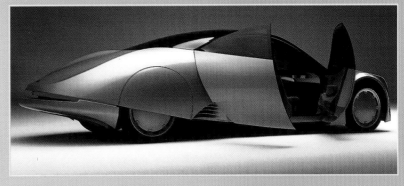

△ The Ford *Synergy* is a prototype vehicle driven by hybrid propulsion. It could be in production by 2010.

△ By making cars lighter, they can be made more fuel-efficient and, in the case of the McClaren *F1*, much faster. This supercar has a lightweight carbon fiber body shell.

A host of extras

Despite joystick-controlled prototypes, the steering wheel is likely to remain a part of cars in the future. However, steering and other driver tasks, such as navigation, braking, and gear changing, will benefit from advances in onboard computer systems. Drivers will also use voice-activated mapping and route trackers, and their e-mail will be read to them using a speech synthesizer.

Best of both worlds

Hybrid propulsion offers a compromise between clean, electric-powered cars and high-performance, gasoline models. The electric motor, which gives off no emissions, is operated in built-up areas and at low speeds. On the open road, away from urban areas, the gasoline engine takes over. Hybrid cars cause up to ten times less pollution than conventional cars and are expected to be a popular type of vehicle by 2010.

BLURRED VISION

Predictions that self-driving vehicles would take to the roads by 2000 were wide of the mark. However, in the near future, powerful sensors and more effective control systems will help drivers and make road trips safer.

ON THE ROAD

△ During the 1900s, many cities suffered from serious road congestion. This scene from 1912 shows a traffic jam in the center of London.

By 2015, a growing number of cities and towns will encourage the use of bikes, electric-powered, single-person vehicles, and new mass-transit initiatives. However, the most extensive change to road transportation will be Intelligent Traffic Systems (ITS). By 2020, ITS may be in use in the U.S., Japan, and Europe. ITS use computer networks to manage traffic, keep vehicles a set distance apart, and advise drivers on the best routes. Its advocates promise less congested roads, a reduction in accidents, and huge savings in fuel consumption because of more efficient route planning.

Traffic management

Advanced Intelligent Traffic Systems will be based on a sophisticated network of sensors. These will map an entire road journey and communicate with computers in the car. By 2025, cars may travel in a convoy, each car's speed and distance from other vehicles being controlled automatically in a system called platooning.

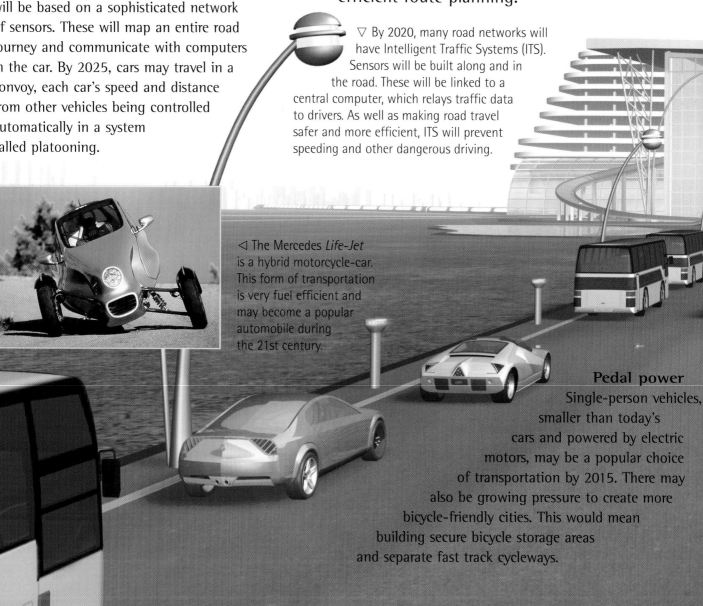

▽ By 2020, many road networks will have Intelligent Traffic Systems (ITS). Sensors will be built along and in the road. These will be linked to a central computer, which relays traffic data to drivers. As well as making road travel safer and more efficient, ITS will prevent speeding and other dangerous driving.

◁ The Mercedes Life-Jet is a hybrid motorcycle-car. This form of transportation is very fuel efficient and may become a popular automobile during the 21st century.

Pedal power

Single-person vehicles, smaller than today's cars and powered by electric motors, may be a popular choice of transportation by 2015. There may also be growing pressure to create more bicycle-friendly cities. This would mean building secure bicycle storage areas and separate fast track cycleways.

Self diagnosis

By 2010, many cars will be built with a fully integrated central computer connected to sensors throughout the car. The computer will monitor many aspects of performance, from brake quality to engine timing. The computer will automatically maximize performance and efficiency, warn of potential malfunctions, and communicate directly with a car repair company. Using a system called telemetry, the repair service may even be able to diagnose and fix certain internal faults by remote control.

△ The Urban Dream bicycle is a new type of folding bike that uses lightweight materials to make it easier to carry. These bikes are light enough to carry in one hand and are ideal for commuters to move quickly around cities.

▷ The recumbent bicycle may be a common sight on roads in the future. Cycling in this position places less stress on the body, allowing the cyclist to travel faster for longer distances.

◁ Advanced electronic entertainment will be an optional feature in most automobiles by 2010. Special screens fitted to the seat backs will provide games, movies, and Internet access.

SEA TRANSPORTATION

▷ Until the arrival of steamships in the early 1800s, long-distance sea journeys had to be made on sailing ships. They relied on the wind, which was unpredictable, to move forward.

Sail revival

A new form of a traditional technology is likely to appear on many ships. By 2015, tankers and giant container ships may be fitted with sails to complement the regular engines. The sails will be computer-controlled to take advantage of the wind, regardless of what direction it is blowing. Although this system depends on weather conditions, it can reduce fuel consumption by as much as 25 percent.

It has been almost a century since sea transportation provided the fastest and, in some cases, the only link between distant places. However, shipping continues to be one of the most effective methods of moving goods and materials around the planet. New propulsion systems will help cut transportation times, and this will encourage more industries to move freight by sea. Passenger vessels will also grow in popularity. On short journeys, small ferries can carry people across the water at high speed. At the other end of the scale is a new generation of ocean liners that can carry up to 5,000 people and feature a mall, ice skating rink, and even artificial beaches on board.

▷ This ground-effect craft of the year 2030 skims the surface on a cushion of air created by its giant wings. Ground-effect craft will also be able to cross flat, isolated areas and icy wastes.

Magnet power

Magnetohydrodynamic (MHD) propulsion could become a common form of sea propulsion by the 2030s. MHD uses a superconducting magnet to generate a powerful electric field around tubes filled with seawater. An electric current passes through the water and generates a strong force that drives the water out of the tubes and the craft forward. MHD has no moving parts, takes up little room, works well at high speeds and creates little noise or vibration. MHD propulsion may power new generations of superfast, short-distance ferries, as well as long-distance cruisers and military "stealth" ships.

◁ The *Yamato 1* is the world's first boat to be powered by magnetohydrodynamic propulsion. Thrust is provided by an electric current that passes through seawater. Future vessels will be capable of speeds up to 55 mph (90km/h).

△ The *Solar Sailor* uses large modules of waterproofed solar cells to provide power. The sails can be tilted at any angle to catch the sunlight as well as the wind.

Flying boats

By 2020, a new kind of vessel that looks —and acts—more like a plane than a ship may be in operation. Ground-effect craft will use the extra lift generated by a wing flying a few feet above the surface of the water to cruise at speeds of up to 280 mph (450km/h). The reduced drag created by this form of propulsion will make these craft extremely fuel efficient. Ground-effect craft will be able to carry very large payloads—or up to 600 passengers—but at a much lower cost than conventional air transportation.

△ Sailing boats are still a popular choice for recreational and sporting activities. Advanced sail systems and computer-controlled weather and navigation systems make these lightweight yachts safer and extremely maneuverable.

▷ The *Carnival Destiny*, built in 1996, can carry over 2,500 passengers in great luxury. It is as long as three football fields and, at 184 feet (56m), is taller than the Statue of Liberty.

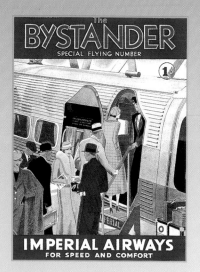

IMPERIAL AIRWAYS
FOR SPEED AND COMFORT

◁ During the 1930s, air travel was a luxury that only the wealthy could afford. Aircraft seated small numbers of people and usually had to land and refuel nearly every 200 miles (400km).

AIRPORTS AND AIR TRAVEL

The number of air passengers is expected to triple over the first twenty years of the 21st century, placing enormous demands on airports around the world. Many airports are already at their full capacity. Building more runways is not the answer because city locations and crowded airspace mean there is little room for further expansion. One solution is to build bigger airliners and new airports. Floating airports are another possibility, as is the use of land reclaimed from the sea. However, the most radical changes to airports are likely to take place inside the passenger terminals.

▷ In the future, faster processing of passengers and more reliable aircraft will help prevent unnecessary delays and overcrowded scenes such as this one at Gatwick Airport in England.

Smoother procedures

Automated passenger handling systems will remove many of the lengthy administration procedures that affect air travelers today. By 2010, advanced imaging systems and powerful computers will mean that procedures such as passport control and security checks can be performed automatically, without the delays caused by human intervention. Time spent on the ground will be significantly reduced and this in turn will help reduce overcrowding in terminals.

△ Electronic tagging will ensure your baggage never gets lost. Screens built into the casing will display all relevant flight information.

◁ Electronic passport control, as well as body and baggage checks, will be performed by a single walk-through scanner system. This will allow faster departures and arrivals.

▽ Some airlines have already introduced automated ticket dispensers that reduce check-in, ticketing and boarding times.

Local air transportation

Short flights from city to city or even within a metropolitan area are likely to receive a major boost by 2010 with the arrival of fleets of tilt-rotor aircraft. These aircraft are capable of short and vertical takeoffs and landings because they can tilt their turboshaft engines upward. For regular flight, the engines are returned to a horizontal position. With cruise speeds of around 300 mph (500km/h), tilt-rotor aircraft are faster, quieter, and more fuel-efficient than helicopters.

Cabin flexibility

In the early years of the 21st century, air travelers can expect to see two new trends. For short flights, some aircraft will be designed without cargo holds, but with larger cabin storage instead. These fast-track flights will offer quick, regular services for walk-on, walk-off passengers. For long-distance flights, travelers who can afford it will have their own private sleeping cabins. These will be constructed with foldaway beds and ceiling storage to maximize space.

△ Hong Kong Airport opened in 1998. Its main terminal is nearly a mile long, has driverless trains, and 54 moving walkways. The airport can handle up to 87 million passengers a year.

AIRLINERS

Aircraft have come a long way since the first wood and canvas contraptions took to the air at the beginning of the 1900s. Air travel has transformed millions of people's lives by making it possible to travel abroad or make long journeys, which in the past would have taken days or even months. Aircraft will become faster and continue to grow in size, some carrying up to a thousand passengers at a time. Long-range aircraft that do not need to refuel will cut traveling time on longhaul flights by up to a third. But the most exciting proposals are for high-speed airliners that use rocket engines to blast the craft into space.

△ The de Havilland Comet was the world's first jet airliner. It began passenger service in 1952 and could carry 36 passengers.

Increased capacity

In 1997, there were over 1.6 billion air travelers. This figure is expected to rise to over 5 billion by 2020. To cope with the additional demand, larger aircraft will be built for the more popular routes. Two-tiered airliners carrying up to 700 passengers will be in service by 2020 and 900-seat models by 2030. Airports and boarding procedures will also have to be radically altered to cope with the rapid increase in passenger numbers.

△ The Airbus Industries A3XX is expected to be in service by 2006. This new type of mega-jumbo will seat 555 passengers and have a range of over 8,000 miles (14,000km). Future versions will carry over 650 people.

The pursuit of speed

The first supersonic aircraft began flying regular passenger services in the 1970s. The Concorde can fly at speeds of 1,488 mph (2,400km/h)—almost three times the speed of conventional aircraft. The next generation of high-speed craft will be be hypersonic, flying at Mach 5 and above (Concorde cruises just above Mach 2). Some hypersonic designs will be suborbital—powerful rocket engines will boost the aircraft into partial orbit around the earth. The aircraft will then glide down to its destination.

▽▷ Hypersoar will use its engines to fly to the edge of the earth's atmosphere and into space. It will then shut down its engines and glide down to an altitude of 25 miles (40km) before firing its engines again. This trajectory prevents it overheating in the extremely hot atmosphere. Hypersoar will carry passengers to the other side of the world in under two hours.

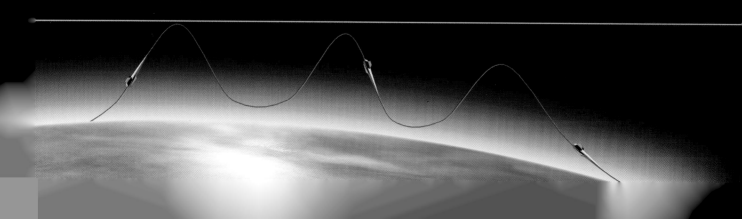

One of the most revolutionary proposals for future aircraft design is the Hypersoar craft. Hypersoar will skim the top of the earth's atmosphere in a unique skipping trajectory, operating its engines in short bursts. It will fly and coast back to earth at speeds of up to 6,200 mph (10,000km/h). By 2035, Hypersoar aircraft could be in operation flying express mail and special services. Larger, passenger-carrying craft may be launched five or ten years later.

▷ The X-34 reusable rocket is likely to be the successor to the space shuttle. Some of its technology is likely to be used in suborbital and hypersonic airliners.

At the beginning of the 1900s some people envisaged that a constant traffic of flying machines would fill the skies. Here, flying taxis and private craft hover and fly above Paris.

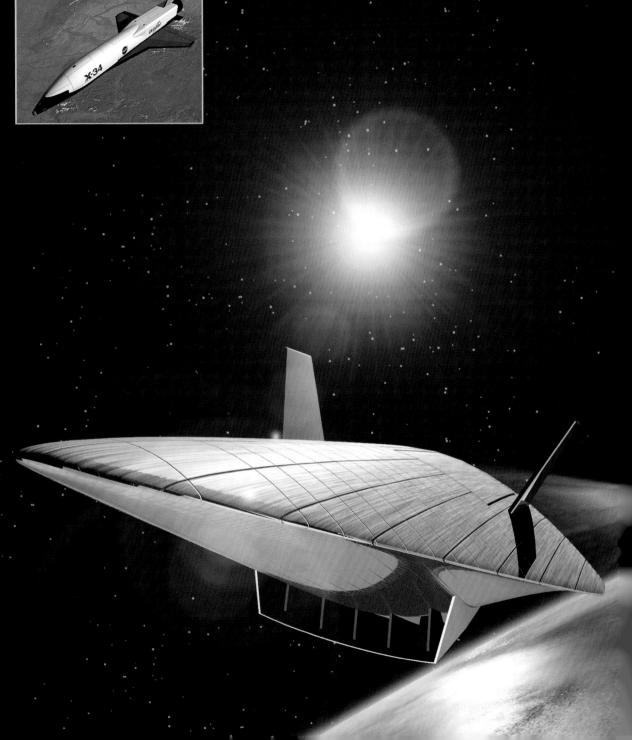

1760s
Industrial Revolution in Great Britain changes the way people work

1800s
Development of organized rules for many sports

1870s
First practical typewriters used in offices

1938
Photocopy machines appear

1950
First credit cards in use

1960s
Cost of air travel plummets—air travel now available to many people

1980s
Arrival of affordable personal computers

WORK AND PLAY

In the last two decades of the twentieth century, computers and new technology dramatically changed the the way we work and live. The Information Revolution will continue to transform society in almost every area, from education to recreational pursuits. Full-time jobs will become increasingly scarce with a growing number of people doing part-time work. Many offices will close as people work from home, linked by videophones, teleconferencing, and intelligent computer networks a thousand times faster than the current Internet. The search for work will involve scouring the whole globe, not just the local area. When not working, you will be able to visit local artificial resorts, climate-controlled by technology to mimic more distant and exotic locations. However, as everyday environments become increasingly secure and controlled, some people will seek thrills by pursuing new adrenaline-inducing sports.

2060
Machines directly controlled by the mind

2040
First vacations in orbiting space hotels

2010s
Huge increase in telecommuting

THE WAY TO WORK

Today we are living in the early years of the Information Revolution. The number of people in manufacturing industries will continue to go down—by 2025, less than two percent of the workforce in the developed world will work in factories. Jobs that involve computers and communications will continue to increase. Other major growth areas will include tourism and professional care for an increasingly aging population. Many jobs were once for life. In the future, most employment will be short-term, away from a fixed base, and will rely on technology to link workers and customers.

△ In the early part of the 1900s, working conditions in offices were often cramped and uncomfortable.

△▷ By 2010, wearable computers will provide complete office facilities for workers on the move. An alternative to the office-on-the-arm system uses a headset to create the illusion of a full-size computer screen.

Telecommuting

Many people already work from home. In the future, telecommuting will continue to grow, affecting millions of workers, from technical support staff to salespeople. Links to customers and coworkers will be provided by high-speed data networks, multiline telephone systems, and real-time, high-quality video cameras. Computers could even be used to measure aspects of an employee's work performance.

◁ A laptop computer linked to a modem and satellite mobile phone allows people working in the most isolated areas to keep in touch with colleagues almost anywhere in the world.

▽ Many meetings in the workplace of the future are likely to use advanced communications, such as this 3-D holographic system, to bring people together. Holography uses lasers to produce lifelike images.

Flexible workers

Current work trends such as short-term contracts, more women in work, and more part-time jobs will continue well into the 21st century. It is estimated that by 2010, more than 40 percent of the workforce will be women. Despite the growth of teleworking, however, not everyone will operate from home—a significant part of the workforce will become much more mobile. Fewer international barriers and restrictions will allow more people to travel abroad in a global search for different kinds of work.

Future offices

Although more people will work at home, offices will not disappear. Many will evolve into communication centers for employees to use. The buildings will become spaces for workers on the move, and the offices will be highly flexible. Staff will find themselves hotdesking—using whatever desk is available when they come into work. Smart desks with built-in global communications and computer and copying facilities will recognize and respond to each user.

◁ VR technology will be used increasingly in the design and testing of products before they are built. Here, engineers and technicians are studying the construction of a car.

△ Teleconferencing uses real-time cameras to provide instant visual communication with people in different places. By 2020, teleconferencing will become more realistic with a new generation of holographic systems.

In the Information Age, knowledge is power. The ability to access information, understand it, and communicate it to others has become highly prized. Education will play a central role in developing these skills. On-line teaching, virtual classrooms, and electronic books (ebooks) will be an essential part of education by the 2020s. Virtual teachers will be increasingly available to many preschool children. Traditional elements of school life, such as group activities, field trips, and printed books, will not disappear altogether, but they may be eclipsed by technological alternatives.

△ In the early part of the 1900s, teaching in many schools relied on strict discipline and inflexible learning techiques.

FUTURE LEARNING

The end of print?

The arrival of affordable ebooks may revolutionize how we read. Ebooks are electronic versions of books and magazines downloaded from the Internet that can be stored and read on a regular PC or on a special, lightweight, handheld reading device. The reading devices can hold thousands of book pages in their memory. Ebooks waste no paper, but still allow users to scribble notes on the text with electronic pens. By 2050, printed books may become collector's items.

School days

By 2030, students might spend more time working from home. Structured classes will use 3-D holographic projection systems, while high-speed data links will enable teachers and students to hold teleconferences. However, time spent interacting with other students at school will continue to be an important part of education.

△ Every generation can benefit from learning with computers. The ability to have interactive classes over the Internet may revolutionize education during the 21st century.

▷ Learning how to use a computer is becoming one of the basic skills for children in the early years of education.

◁ Books still offer unique advantages over computers. They are cheap, portable, and provide easy access to information. However, in the next few decades, books may be replaced by ebooks.

Continuous education

In the future, education will not end when you are 18 or 21. In the rapidly changing Information Age, learning will become a lifelong process. People will need to acquire many new skills during their lifetime. Adults may work on three or more degrees, while learning aids accessed by computers will provide introductions to new subjects and instant updating sessions for many skills.

▷ Interactive displays are fun and important ways of learning at many zoos, museums, and wildlife parks. At the London Aquarium, the public is encouraged to interact with some of the marine life.

△ Virtual reality headsets and data gloves may feature in many schools and homes by 2020. VR can help explain complex topics, such as the atomic structure of elements, in an exciting and effective way.

△ At the end of the 1800s, Egypt had become a destination for wealthy tourists. Mass tourism, however, only emerged with the arrival of cheap airfares in the 1960s.

In the time that it takes you to read this sentence, over 3,000 people will be on a flight to travel to another country—some for business, but most for pleasure. Travel and tourism are the world's biggest industries, generating almost 12 percent of the global income. By 2025, the number of tourists is expected to double, and at least four million new jobs in the travel and tourism industry will be created each year. There will also be a greater range of vacation options. Traditional destinations will remain popular, but people will also be offered new travel opportunities, such as vacations underwater and in space.

TOURISM AND TRAVEL

▽ Scuba divers are just one of the sights you can expect to see from your bedroom window in this underwater hotel off the coast of Florida.

Travel trends

In the future there will be fewer travel agents. This sector will suffer because of the ease and convenience of buying flights and accommodations directly over the Internet. Another technological innovation is likely to be in-ear translation systems. By 2020, an earpiece and tiny microphone will be able to translate most foreign languages in real-time with 90 percent accuracy.

New locations

Despite environmental pressures, it is likely that hotels will be built in the Arctic and Antarctic by 2025. By the middle of the 21st century, space hotels orbiting the earth may be a popular, though expensive, destination. Long before then, we can expect to see a boom in underwater resorts in seas and oceans. All these new destinations will rely on technology to create a comfortable and safe environment for the tourists.

Late in the 21st century, tourists may be able to choose destinations that lie beyond the earth. Water, found frozen in rocks on the moon, may be used as a source for a moon hotel and base.

Access denied

Although tourism generates a large amount of wealth, it can also create a number of problems. Tourism can damage the environment and threaten culturally important sites. The potentially destructive effects caused by a greater number of tourists could lead to a rise in environmental protests, and many historical sites may be closed to the public.

▷ Since the 1990s, there has been an increased demand for unconventional vacations. Antarctica and other protected wilderness areas are becoming established destinations for high-paying tourists.

◁ By 2010, underwater hotels will operate in popular vacation areas, such as the Caribbean, Hawaii, and the South Pacific. Tourist submersibles will ferry people to and from hotels, as well as taking them on seabed sightseeing trips.

LEISURE ACTIVITIES

△ Soccer fans in the 1890s were crammed together in the open. Sports stadiums in the 21st century will offer a range of comforts and features, like LCD screens fitted into seats.

Predictions of a world in which most people are freed from work and household drudgery so that they can live a life of complete leisure are not likely to become a reality during the 21st century. Even so, the amount of free time available to many people will increase because of shorter working hours, less commuting, labor-saving household devices, and services such as Internet shopping. Many traditional activities, including sports, will continue. But we can also expect virtual reality (VR) simulators, sophisticated interactive television, and the creation of new, indoor artificial environments.

◁ This three-dimensional version of the Spiderman cartoon character thrills visitors at Universal Studios in Orlando. Future VR systems will offer a greater level of realism and interaction.

◁ Giant fans generate wind conditions of up to 25 knots in this wind-surfing arena in Paris, France. Future sport centers will produce even more lifelike conditions.

▽ *Sarcos* is a robot capable of recognizing and reacting to a human table tennis player's moves. Robotic opponents are likely to become a popular feature of future game centers.

Inside the dome

Not all recreational time will be spent at home. You may be able to visit an exotic location just a short journey from where you live. During the 21st century, we can expect to see a rise in the popularity of recreational domes. Such structures already exist in Japan. They recreate a variety of environments, like tropical beaches or winter resorts. The weather outdoors is never a problem because the domes are completely self-contained and maintain a constant climate.

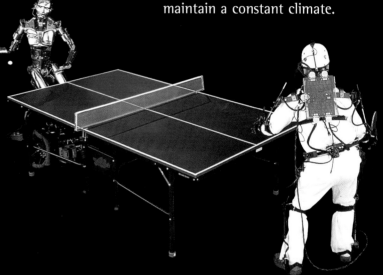

Stay at home

Future homes, equipped with the latest technology, may be the place where millions of people choose to spend their recreational time. Exercise machines that simulate outdoor activities will be a common feature as people spend more time indoors. Entertainment systems will become increasingly interactive. For example, you will probably be able to watch sporting events from a number of different camera angles or choose your own instant replays.

Another world

Virtual reality (VR), which generates a realistic three-dimensional world around a person, has the potential to revolutionize games and entertainment. By 2015, today's cumbersome VR helmets are likely to be replaced by lightweight displays or glasses that project images directly into the eye. By 2025, VR bodysuits will create a new level of realism by using a system of sensors and tiny mechanical devices that simulate all the senses.

▷ The Seagaia Ocean resort complex in Miyazaki, Japan, is the world's most advanced all-weather indoor resort. It can hold 10,000 visitors.

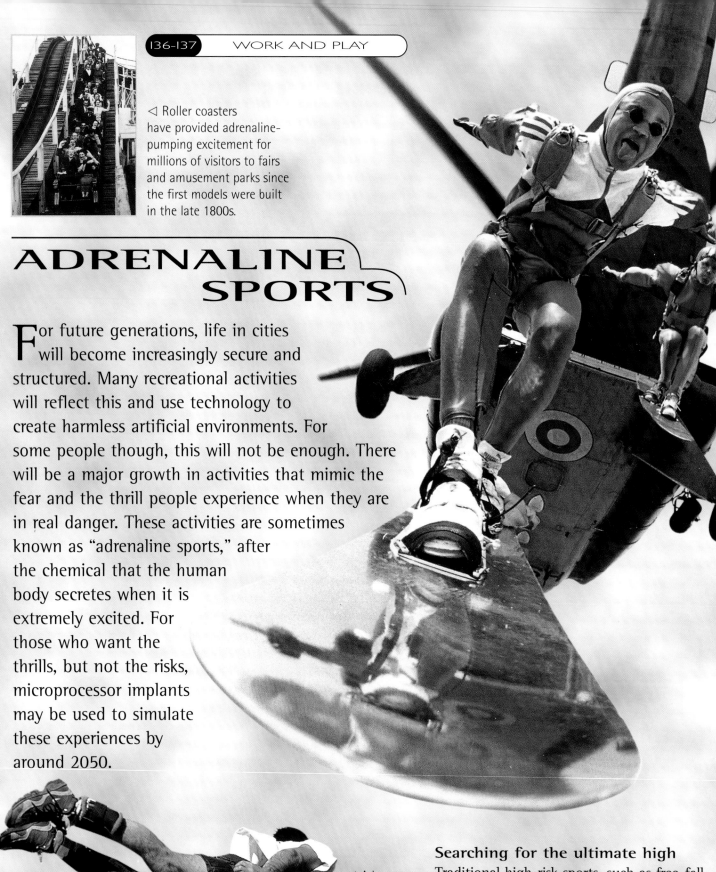

◁ Roller coasters have provided adrenaline-pumping excitement for millions of visitors to fairs and amusement parks since the first models were built in the late 1800s.

ADRENALINE SPORTS

For future generations, life in cities will become increasingly secure and structured. Many recreational activities will reflect this and use technology to create harmless artificial environments. For some people though, this will not be enough. There will be a major growth in activities that mimic the fear and the thrill people experience when they are in real danger. These activities are sometimes known as "adrenaline sports," after the chemical that the human body secretes when it is extremely excited. For those who want the thrills, but not the risks, microprocessor implants may be used to simulate these experiences by around 2050.

◁ A bungee jumper, attached only by a strong, elastic rope, free-falls through the air. The rope pulls jumpers back before they hit the ground.

Searching for the ultimate high
Traditional high-risk sports, such as free-fall parachuting, spelunking, and climbing, will continue to attract people looking for an element of danger in their recreational activities. Newer, extreme sports and activities will also evolve—including illegal ones such as hangliding from the tops of tall buildings.

▷ River rapids make white-water rafting a dangerous, though exciting, activity. Rafts are usually inflatable and made of tough nylon fabric. White-water rafting will continue to grow in popularity over the next decade.

Safe fighting

While organized sports provide an outlet for some people's violent feelings, a new breed of aggression-releasing activities will be developed during the 21st century. Impact-resistant headguards and bodysuits will allow people to fight and wrestle without the risk of physical injury. Virtual reality bodysuits will also be in use by 2020. They will enable people to battle each other or a computer-generated opponent from the safety of an arcade or their own homes.

◁ Sky-surfers surf the air on specially adapted snowboards before opening their parachutes and dropping to the ground. We can expect to see a growth in these kinds of hybrid sports as people seek new challenges.

▽ Street lugers ride on lightweight boards mounted on low-friction wheels that can reach speeds of up to 80 mph (130km/h). A more extreme version, bodyblading, in which the wheels are attached directly to a bodysuit, could provide a new activity for adrenaline seekers during the 21st century.

All in the mind

One day, microprocessor-controlled implants may simulate adrenaline highs even more realistically than third- or fourth-generation virtual reality systems. By 2040, surgical implants in the skull may use biofeedback to both record and shape thought patterns in the brain.

2050
Cloud seeding machines used to create rain

2020
Human body parts—grown in animals—are available

2010
Common medicines are grown in plants with biotechnology

2000
Draft map of the human genome project completed.

HEALTHY LIVING

During the 21st century, people will live longer and lead healthier lives than ever before. Improved health care, breakthroughs in the understanding of the human body, and even the possibility of developing "spare" body parts will improve the lives of millions of people. Advances in genetics will allow doctors to screen and treat people—even babies still in the womb—for many diseases that are currently incurable. Major developments are also expected in biotechnology and farming. Increases in food production, combined with more effective water management, have the potential to prevent the terrible famines and droughts that afflicted many developing nations during the 1900s. The cost of good health care, an increasingly aging population, and providing enough food and water worldwide will dominate the politics of many countries over the next century.

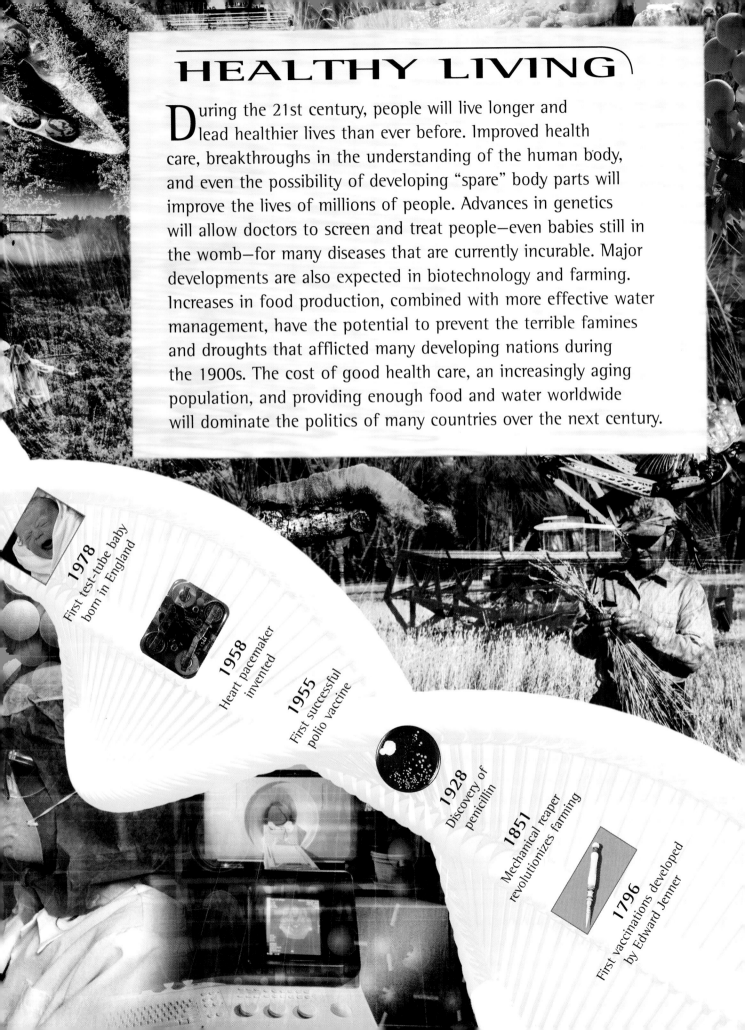

1978 First test-tube baby born in England

1958 Heart pacemaker invented

1955 First successful polio vaccine

1928 Discovery of penicillin

1851 Mechanical reaper revolutionizes farming

1796 First vaccinations developed by Edward Jenner

△ Freshwater was not readily available for most people before the 1900s. Today, in some countries, many people still do not have access to water in their homes.

In developed nations, clean water, waste disposal, and sanitation are often taken for granted—until there are water shortages or blockages in pipes and drains. For millions of people in developing nations, however, this is not the case. For them, sanitation and access to clean water can mean the difference between life and death. During the 21st century, new techniques in supplying and generating water, combined with improvements in weather forecasting, will have a global benefit.

WEATHER, WATER, AND WASTE

△ Global warming may become partly responsible for major droughts during the 21st century. These will put a great strain on the world's water supplies.

The big issues
Although freshwater is abundant on a global scale, it is often scarce locally. It has been estimated that over a billion people around the world lack access to safe water. More effective and fairer distribution of water will become a priority during the 21st century. Governments should ensure that existing water supplies, such as rivers, do not become contaminated as a result of pollution.

Disposal
Over 7 gallons (30l) of freshwater are used each time a toilet is flushed. Waste needs to be removed, but alternatives that use as little water as possible in the process need to be found. Waterless toilets, which use layers of bacteria in sealed tanks to digest waste and turn it into harmless compost, are one possibility. They require no water and prevent the spread of disease.

◁ Huge quantities of industrial waste, called effluent, are poured into rivers, polluting water supplies. If this continues, many valuable sources of freshwater will become unsuitable for human consumption, even after treatment at water purification plants..

◁ Desalination plants use up large amounts of energy, but are capable of turning salt water into freshwater. Future plants may be considerably more energy efficient.

Freshwater for all

In areas where water is scarce, efforts may turn to water generation rather than collection and distribution. Cost-effective extraction of freshwater from salt water at desalination plants may be likely in the near future. By 2050, altering the chemical structure of clouds, or cloud seeding, may be used to make rain where it is needed most.

△ The Meteosat weather satellite, built by the European Space Agency, transmits an image of cloud patterns back to a ground base on earth every 30 minutes.

◁ By the middle of the 21st century, vast fleets of insect-sized cloud seeding machines, or mesicopters, may be launched in areas with little rainfall. Once inside the clouds, the mesicopters will release chemical particles that cause water vapor to form and fall as rain.

▷ The development of new materials and advances in microengineering will allow the manufacture of cheap and extremely small machines.

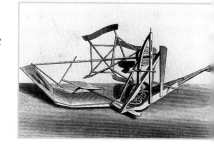

▷ The mechanical reaping machine, invented by Cyrus Hall McCormick in 1851, allowed farmers to quadruple the amount of grain they could harvest.

FUTURE FARMING

For thousands of years, most of the world's population farmed the land. Crops were grown and animals were raised to support each family. Any surplus was taken to the market to be sold. During the 1700s, the Agricultural Revolution in Europe began a process that continues today—a small proportion of people produce food for the majority. During the 21st century, technology, including "smart" harvesting machinery, biotechnology, and hydroponics, will make farming more efficient. Even so, it will take a great deal of political action, as well as scientific advances, to end global hunger.

△ These Atlantic salmon are being farmed in Norway—10 percent of seafood is farmed in this way. This figure is likely to triple by 2025.

▷ It is likely that droughts and famines will continue long into the 21st century. Millions of people, like these refugees in Zaire, will rely on food aid from other countries to survive.

▷ Tea leaf pickers on an Indonesian plantation are likely to remain in work for decades to come. It will be a long time before robots and machines will be capable of harvesting such delicate crops.

Unequal world

One of the great inequalities of the modern world is that, while some countries produce an amount of food surplus to their needs, millions still go hungry and die from starvation or malnutrition each year. This is likely to continue unless governments around the world take the initiative and there is a shift in attitudes. It is also hoped that food production levels can be raised by biotechnology, advances in pest control, and the creation of crops that can survive droughts and other weather extremes.

◁ In this greenhouse, a computer controlled watering unit provides the exact amount of water required for maximum plant growth.

▷ Killing pests, such as slugs, can involve using dangerous chemical pesticides that dissolve into the soil. This pest control robot can collect and eradicate pests without using chemicals. Once caught, the slugs are turned into a biogas, which then powers the robot.

Popular science has predicted that a person's nutritional needs will be found in a single pill. Although it may be possible, the benefits and enjoyment of eating a variety of foods means that it is unlikely to replace our current diet.

Robo-farmers

Farming is time-consuming, labor-intensive work. In developed nations, farming is a mechanized process. Many machines are used, from combine harvesters to crop sorters and packaging devices in factories. Future technology will be developed to increase production and reduce costs. By 2025, robots will probably tend delicate greenhouse plants, such as tomatoes, as well as harvest fruit crops. More automation will also be used in the rearing of livestock.

Farming fish

Fish and other sea products are a major source of protein. By 2015, worldwide demand for all forms of seafood is expected to increase by 50 percent. To meet this demand, the fishing industry will need to exploit new fishing grounds and invest more in aquaculture, or fish farming. Aquaculture takes place in lakes, ponds, and reservoirs, where the environment can be carefully controlled.

▷ Hydroponics may become an important branch of farming. Hydroponics is the growing of plants without using soil. This researcher is studying lettuce and tomato plants in a laboratory in Arizona.

◁▷ Biotechnology has the power to create uniquely patterned flowers, as well as the potential for more important uses, like longer lasting fruit and vegetables, or the creation of new medicines derived from plants, or even animals.

BIOTECHNOLOGY

Biotechnology is the name given to techniques used to control living organisms for the benefit of humans. Although it is linked in many people's minds with the genetic engineering of plants and animals in order to create new, hybrid species, this is only one part of the biotechnology story. Biotechnology has the potential to eradicate food shortages, to cure many diseases, and to produce eco-friendly fuels and materials. However, the debate about whether we should be tampering with nature will continue for some time.

Food supplies

People have been selecting seeds, growing plant hybrids, and interbreeding animals for centuries to produce more robust crops and livestock. Biotechnology could increase the amounts of crops worldwide. Damage inflicted by pests and diseases, as well as spoiling at farms, packaging factories, and stores, means that as much as half of all fruits and vegetables grown never become available to the consumer. By creating longer lasting, disease resistant products, food production could receive an enormous boost by 2015.

△ A great part of biotechnology work on plants takes place in laboratories where genetically engineered seedlings can be grown and studied in controlled conditions.

Growing plastics

Plants are likely to provide a major source of materials in the future. In the 1920s starch collected from plants began to be used to produce acetone and other paint solvents. In the future a new form of plastic may be grown and stored within genetically modified plants, such as potatoes. Unlike today's plastic, which is manufactured using expensive and limited oil reserves, this plastic would be cheap to produce and would also be biodegradable.

Medical breakthroughs

Biotechnology has the potential to make radical changes in the way we obtain many important medicines. Turnips, for example, have already been modified to produce anticancer drugs. Another strand of biotechnology called "pharming" uses modified farm animals to generate important substances for the pharmaceutical industry. By 2025, "pharmed" livestock may provide our most important medicines.

△ Advances in biotechnology have resulted in the first self-shearing sheep. The sheep is injected with a special solution, called Bioclip, that contains a protein that causes wool fibers to break away.

▷ A researcher analyzes how a sweet sorghum plant reacts to different watering conditions. Sweet sorghum is a common cereal crop that scientists are studying to determine whether it can become a leading source of biofuel in the 21st century.

GENETIC ENGINEERING

Genes are the instructions that determine an organism's characteristics. In humans, for example, everything from hair and eye color to susceptibility to certain diseases is passed down, or inherited, from parents via genes. Genes are contained in a chemical called DNA, which is found in the cells of all living things. Identifying and understanding how to manipulate genes is revolutionizing science. Genetic illnesses may one day become a thing of the past. Unborn children may be tested for genetic defects and treated in the womb using a technique called gene therapy. However, the ability to fundamentally alter genes means that there are major concerns about the consequences of genetic engineering.

△ The British scientist Francis Crick and American James Watson discovered the double helix, or spiral, structure of DNA (deoxyribonucleic acid) in 1953.

Cloning

Scientists have been successful in creating identical copies, or clones, of existing plants and animals. In 1997, Dolly the sheep became the first mammal cloned from the cell of another adult mammal. However, cloning has been regarded with some suspicion—the ethics of creating identical humans has been a concern to many, but it is more likely to be used in medical research or to produce higher-yield crops.

◁ These baby mice glow green under a blue light. They have been genetically engineered to include a jellyfish gene that causes them to become fluorescent. The gene may be used to mark and study cancerous cells in humans.

◁ Dolly is a genetic duplicate, or clone. She was created from a cell extracted from an adult sheep.

▷ The Human Genome Project (HGP) is providing a new understanding of our genetic make-up. Four chemicals, known as A, G, C, and T, are found in each gene. Determining their order is a major part of the HGP.

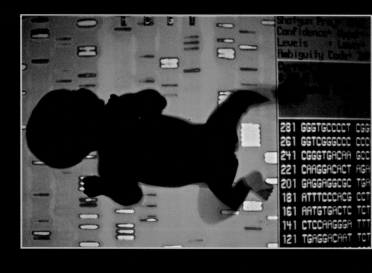

281 GGGTGCCCCT CGG
261 GGTCGGGCCC CCC
241 CGGGTGACAA GCC
221 CAAGGACACT AGA
201 GAGGAGGCGC TGA
181 ATTTCCCACG CCT
161 AATGTGACTC TCT
141 CTCCAAGGGA TTT
121 TGAGGACAAT TCT

▷ The corkscrew-shaped DNA chemical is present in every single cell. DNA stores genes, which are the instructions that determine an organism's traits. Although it can only be seen under an electron microscope, human DNA would stretch over 16 feet (5m) if it was unfolded.

△ Thousands of scientists are working across the world to determine the sequence of the coded information contained in human DNA.

▷ Special growth cells created by genetic engineering will play a major role in growing artificial skin and blood vessels.

Gene therapy

Genetic defects are responsible for almost 5,000 diseases. Gene therapy is a new form of treatment that involves the insertion of a healthy gene into a virus that has been neutralized so that it can do no harm. The modified virus, carrying the corrected gene, is then injected into the patient. In this way, inherited diseases, including hemophilia and cystic fibrosis—the most common genetic disorder in the Western world—may be successfully combated.

CRYSTAL BALL

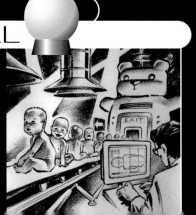

The power to manipulate the genes of unborn children raises the fear of "designer" babies. In the future, unless prevented by law, parents will be able to specify the sex, looks, and even the behavior of their children.

Breaking the code

Begun in 1990, the Human Genome Project is one of the most ambitious and important scientific projects ever undertaken. The draft sequence of the genome was completed in June 2000. It deciphers 3 billion bits of DNA containing our genes and will provide scientists with a revolutionary new tool for diagnosing, treating, and, one day, potentially preventing most human diseases and disorders.

◁ Many doctors once believed that protective clothing would prevent them from catching their patients' illnesses. In the 1600s, doctors became known as "quacks." This came from the Dutch word "quacksalver," a seller of remedies.

FINDING A CURE

Historically, the world's biggest killers have not been wars or natural disasters, but diseases. In 1918, for example, a new strain of influenza virus killed at least 40 million people. During the 1900s, the average life expectancy across the globe increased as we learned more about diseases and how to combat them. Even so, in the first half of the 21st century medical research will face some major challenges. These will include an increase of certain diseases as populations age, and the possibility of new viruses and superbugs that are immune to conventional treatments.

◁ A woman from northern India is injected with a vaccine against tetanus. Vaccinating people has been one of the greatest victories in the fight against disease.

△ The smart pill, unlike other oral medicines, will target a specific area of the body. After the pill has been swallowed, its path through the digestive system will be traced by radio signals. Once the pill has reached its destination (in this case a growth in the large intestine) a signal will be sent to release the drugs.

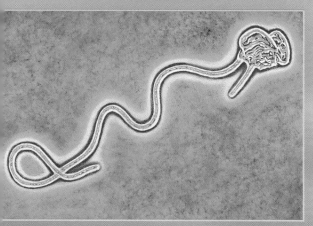

◁ The deadly Ebola virus, shown here at 19,000x magnification, is responsible for fever and, frequently, rapid death. Scientists must find new ways of treating such diseases. In many cases the overuse of antibiotics has created viruses that are drug-resistant.

Making the medicine go down

In the future, doctors will be able to tailor specific medicines for each patient with much greater effectiveness. Genetic testing will help determine exact dosages and reduce side effects. Some medicines will be sprayed onto edible strips of paper, while others will be dispensed in smart pills. Controlled by microelectronics, smart pills will target a specific area of the body before releasing their cargo of medicine.

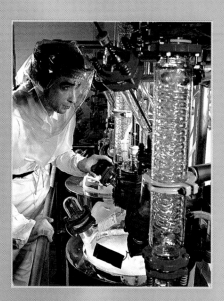

▷ Finding effective ways of dispensing medicines is an important aspect of medical research. This technician is testing a medicine that can be delivered by a simple spray system.

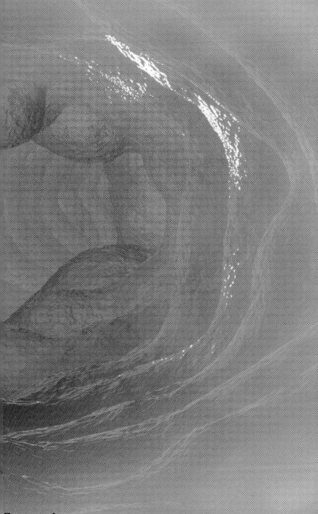

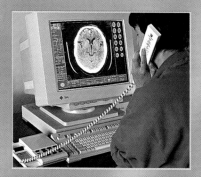

◁ A radiologist studies a patient's brain scan, which has been sent through a telephone line. Telemedicine may be used increasingly to allow specialists to make a diagnosis from almost anywhere in the world.

Screening

Preventive medicine and early diagnosis are the keys to reducing the number of premature deaths. Today's PET and MRI scanners will be joined by even more powerful screening tools that can peer into the body and detect potential problems and diseases much earlier. These include laser probes that can identify precancerous cells with extreme accuracy, and holographic medical imaging that will provide a three-dimensional view inside the body.

Prevention

As life expectancy increases, so does the likelihood of developing certain diseases, including many cancers, heart disease, and diabetes. Our genetic makeup plays a major, but not exclusive, role in determining whether or not we become sick. During the 21st century there will be a greater emphasis on maintaining a healthy lifestyle in order to prevent disease. Diet, exercise, and low stress levels will be promoted as the most important factors for a long and healthy life.

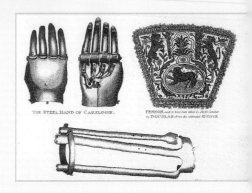

▷ During the 1800s, artificial limbs were very cumbersome and offered little flexibility. This 1815 engraving shows a steel hand and the metal frame that held it in place.

REPAIRING OUR BODIES

△ It takes only three weeks to grow just over one square yard of artificial skin from a tiny fragment. Artificial skin is used mainly to help burn victims.

Until the second half of the 20th century, when people lost a limb the most they could hope for was a crude, clumsy replacement. If a major internal organ such as the heart failed, recovery was rare. Since the 1960s, there have been advances in surgery, tissue engineering, artifical parts technology, and transplant operations. These developments have saved millions of lives and improved the quality of life for countless others. Further breakthroughs will mean that by 2025, most of your body—both inside and out—can be repaired, or damaged parts replaced.

▷ Human cartilage cells have been grafted onto the back of a hairless mouse in an attempt to grow a replica of a human ear.

Robotic assistance

Robots are capable of much greater precision and accuracy than human hands and will play an increasingly important role in surgery. The majority of robots will work as surgical assistants, controlled by surgeons. By 2020, computer networks will allow surgeons to operate remotely by controlling robots and other telesurgery machines from a distance.

Tissue engineering

Currently, the demand for human body parts, especially internal organs, is higher than the supply. This will change, however, with advances in tissue engineering. This area of medical technology works to create tissues—and even new body parts—from human cells. Scientists have been successful growing skin, pieces of bone, and cartilage from human cells. Internal organs may be available by 2030. Known as neo-organs, these will be grown in laboratory conditions, or even in animals acting as living hosts.

▷ MRI devices are powerful body imaging systems that have been beneficial to surgery and body repair. MRI stands for Magnetic Resonance Imaging and the devices produce detailed images of cross sections of the human body.

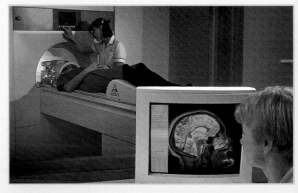

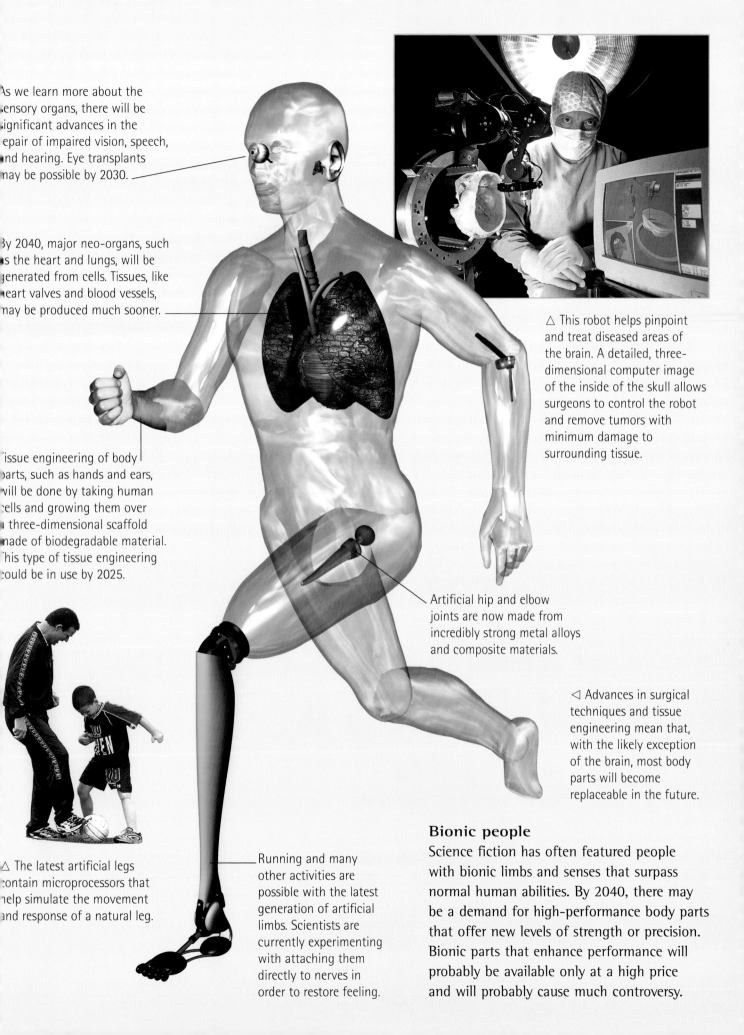

As we learn more about the sensory organs, there will be significant advances in the repair of impaired vision, speech, and hearing. Eye transplants may be possible by 2030.

By 2040, major neo-organs, such as the heart and lungs, will be generated from cells. Tissues, like heart valves and blood vessels, may be produced much sooner.

Tissue engineering of body parts, such as hands and ears, will be done by taking human cells and growing them over a three-dimensional scaffold made of biodegradable material. This type of tissue engineering could be in use by 2025.

△ The latest artificial legs contain microprocessors that help simulate the movement and response of a natural leg.

△ This robot helps pinpoint and treat diseased areas of the brain. A detailed, three-dimensional computer image of the inside of the skull allows surgeons to control the robot and remove tumors with minimum damage to surrounding tissue.

Artificial hip and elbow joints are now made from incredibly strong metal alloys and composite materials.

◁ Advances in surgical techniques and tissue engineering mean that, with the likely exception of the brain, most body parts will become replaceable in the future.

Running and many other activities are possible with the latest generation of artificial limbs. Scientists are currently experimenting with attaching them directly to nerves in order to restore feeling.

Bionic people

Science fiction has often featured people with bionic limbs and senses that surpass normal human abilities. By 2040, there may be a demand for high-performance body parts that offer new levels of strength or precision. Bionic parts that enhance performance will probably be available only at a high price and will probably cause much controversy.

◁ Until the 20th century, people across the world frequently died in childhood. In this painting from the 1880s, a mother tends to her sick daughter.

In the early 1900s, the average person in the United States and Europe was not expected to live beyond 45 years. A person born in a developed country at the beginning of the 21st century can hope to live for twice as long. Advances in medicine and improvements in diet and lifestyle have been—and will continue to be—the key to longer life expectancy. Research into our genetic makeup may even one day enable us to slow down the aging process. For the forseeable future, however, it is likely that the gap between the life expectancies of the developing and developed nations will remain.

HOLDING BACK THE YEARS

Rise of the old

An increasing aging population will have a profound effect on society. It is predicted that the number of retired people will double by 2020, and caring for the elderly will become one of the biggest industries. Because people will remain active for longer, society will find new ways to use their skills. Political parties may be formed to represent this growing and powerful section of the population.

The aging process

Some scientists believe that there is a maximum age that human beings can reach. Others think that there is no natural limit and that locating the genes responsible for aging in humans is the key to a much longer life. Scientists have successfully used genetic engineering to increase the length of life of simple organisms, such as worms and fruit flies. But it is still too early to tell if this will work in the more complex human body.

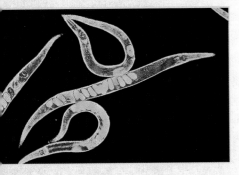

△ Nematode worms have been the focus of extensive research into genetic engineering. It has been shown that modified worms without a particular gene age more slowly than those with the gene.

◁ In parts of Mongolia there is an unusually high proportion of people who are over 100 years old. Careful study of such people can help scientists to discover the connections between long life and lifestyle and, maybe one day, specific genes that control aging.

Coming back from the dead

One possible way of defeating death is cryonics. This involves deep-freezing a person's body soon after death in the hope that advances in medical technology will allow that individual to be revived in the future. Either the whole body or just the head is immersed in liquid nitrogen at -320°F (-196°C) before the body tissue has had a chance to decay. One of the challenges of this technology will be to restore a fully functioning brain with all its memories still intact.

▷ A number of people with fatal or terminal diseases have paid to be kept frozen in low-temperature capsules after they die. It is hoped that sometime in the future doctors will be able to revive and cure them.

▽ During the 21st century, as life expectancy increases, the number of retired people will continue to rise.

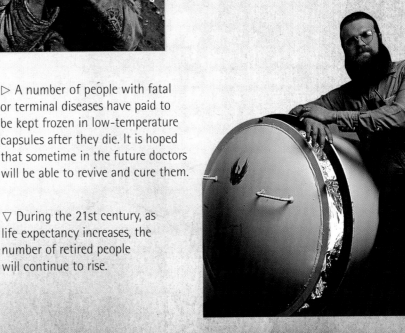

GLOSSARY

Alternative energies
Any source of energy that does not rely on the burning of fossil fuels (gas, coal, and oil) or nuclear power. Alternative energies include solar, geothermal, and hydroelectric power.

Analog
A system or device that handles sound and pictures directly as changing electrical vibrations, rather than by converting them into numbers.
See Digital.

Artificial Intelligence (AI)
The ability of computers and robots to do some of the intelligent things that humans can do, such as thinking, reasoning, and interpreting pictures.

Autonomous
Used to describe a machine, usually a robot, that does not depend on human control to perform all of its functions.

Biometrics
The measurement of a person's unique anatomical features from finger- and handprints to eye and facial characteristics.

Biotechnology
The use of living organisms in industry, agriculture, and science.

Broadband
A communications system that can handle a large amount of information at high speed.

Byte
A unit for measuring the amount of information stored or processed by a computer. There are about 100,000 bytes of text in this book.

Cloning
The process of creating copies of living things from a single cell without sexual reproduction taking place. The new copy, or clone, is physically and genetically identical to the parent cell.

Cloud-seeding
The application of chemicals to clouds in order to generate rain.

Composite materials
Artificial materials that feature a mixture of different materials that are woven or bonded together.

Cryonics
Preserving a dead person's body at -310°F, in the hope that future medical technology will be able to revive it.

Customization
A system of manufacturing items such as cars or clothing in which each individual product is made to suit the requirements of a particular individual.

Digital
A system or device in which sound, pictures, or other information is handled in the form of numbers. The alternative to digital is an analog system.

DNA (Deoxyribonucleic acid)
A complex molecule with a double-helix shape that contains the genetic code for a living organism.

Expert system
Computer software that stores detailed information about a particular subject and uses it to answer questions.

Fiber optics
Long, thin strands of glass through which digital information can be passed in the form of high-speed pulses of laser light.

Force feedback device
Part of a virtual reality setup, which makes users think that they are interacting with solid objects.

Gene therapy
The identification and replacement of genes responsible for certain diseases with healthy genes.

Genetic engineering
The transfer of genes between species to create new organisms that do not occur naturally in nature.

Genome
The sum total of DNA within a species.

Geothermal power
Power generated by using heat that comes from deep inside the earth.

Gravity
The force of attraction between two bodies.

Ground-effect craft
Vehicles, usually seacraft, that have wings to create extra lift. They skim at high speed across flat surfaces.

Holography
A process that uses lasers to produce three-dimensional images.

Hypersonic
Term used for speeds above five times the speed of sound. At sea level the speed of sound is 7,599 mph (1,225km/h).

Information Revolution
The changes in the ways people work and how information is handled; brought on by improvements in computers and telecommunications.

Integrated circuit See Microchip.

Intelligent agent
Software that acts as a personal assistant, helping its user find relevant information on the Internet. Sometimes known as a "knowbot."

Internet
The worldwide network of millions of computers that can communicate with each other.

Invasive surgery
An operation that involves a large cut, or incision, being made in the patient for the doctor to perform surgery.

Knowbot See Intelligent agent.

Laser
A highly focused beam of light or other radiation, used to cut through objects or to carry information through fiber optics.

Magnetic levitation
A method of lifting objects by using magnetic attraction or the forces that keep magnets apart. Using a series of powerful magnets, it is possible for magnetic levitation to propel passenger-carrying trains at speeds of over 279 mph (450km/h).

Magnetohydrodynamic (MHD)
A new method of propulsion for seacraft. Superconducting magnets generate a powerful electric field around thruster tubes filled with seawater.

Mass-transit systems
Transportation systems, such as subways, moving sidewalks, and bus networks, designed to move large numbers of people.

Microchip
A small, but complex electronic device in which millions of transistors and other components are mounted on a single slice of material, usually silicon, to form an integrated circuit.

Microprocessor
A type of microchip that can be programmed to perform calculations or control machinery. Microprocessors are the thinking components in robots and computers.

Nanotechnology
Technology created to work on a nanometric scale. A nanometre is equal to one billionth of a meter.

Neural net
A computer system in which electronic units link to each other in the same way that cells called neurons form a network in the human brain.

Non-invasive surgery
Surgery that relies on medical instruments inserted through a small incision in the patient's body.

Nuclear fission
Splitting the nucleus of an atom to generate enormous amounts of power.

Nuclear fusion
A process that forces atoms to collide and fuse together. This has the potential to generate huge amounts of power. Fusion takes place constantly in the sun's core.

Packet-switching
The way information travels through the Internet, divided into "packets" of data that take different routes for maximum speed and efficiency.

Pharming
The manufacture of medical products, particularly pharmaceutical products, from genetically modified plants or animals. Still in its infancy, this technology could lead to cheap medicines as well as products, such as milk or plants, that contain vaccines against human diseases.

Pneumatics
A drive system that uses a gas, such as air, to provide power.

Quantum computer
A proposed new type of computer that would use particles smaller than atoms to do millions of calculations at once.

Radio
A way of communicating by sending electrical vibrations through space, without using wires or cables.

Radioactivity
The release of electromagnetic energy, or radiation, from the nuclei of unstable atoms.

Recycling
Making productive use of waste substances. For example, making newspaper out of waste paper.

Renewable resources
Materials and energies that can be used without risk of them running out. Examples of renewable resources include solar power, wave power, and crops.

Sensor
A device that provides a computer or microprocessor with environmental information, such as temperature, sound, or light.

SMA (Shape memory alloy)
A new material capable of remembering its original shape and returning to it after being manipulated.

Simulation
Using a computer to imitate the behavior of some other system, such as flying an aircraft or a dangerous situation in a nuclear power plant.

Smart card
A card with a built-in microprocessor that contains personal information and can be used for activities such as shopping and banking.

Smart machine
A machine or system that uses sensors and a microprocessor to make it behave in an intelligent way, for example, by remembering or predicting a user's actions.

Stealth
A collection of technologies that work together to make a vehicle (usually an aircraft) less detectable to radar and other forms of sensing.

Streamlining
The designing and shaping of machines, particularly vehicles such as cars, boats, and aircraft, so that they travel through the water or air more smoothly and efficiently.

Superconductivity
The ability of certain materials to conduct electricity at very low temperatures with little resistance.

Telecommunications
The transmission and reception of information-carrying signals over a long distance. Telephone, radio, and television are familiar telecommunications systems.

Telecomputer
A combined computer and digital television set.

Teleoperation
A system that allows someone to control or operate a machine from a distance.

Telesurgery
The ability to send important medical information over a computer network so that a diagnosis can be made, even though patient and doctor are in different places.

Teleworking
Working from home and using technology, such as computers, the Internet, and fax machines, to stay in touch with a central office and clients.

Terraforming
The modification of the entire environment of a planet and its atmosphere to allow plants and animals from earth to live there.

Tissue engineering
The artificial creation of parts of the body using a variety of techniques.

Transgenic organism
Any living organism that has had its genetic makeup manipulated and altered so that it includes one or more genes from a different species.

Transistor
A tiny electrically-operated switch used in microchips.

Ultrasound
A sensing system that uses very high frequency sounds that are outside the range of human hearing.

Videophone
A telephone whose users can see each other. Also known as a picturephone, or a holophone if it uses holography to produce three-dimensional images.

Virtual reality (VR)
A system that uses computers to generate an artificial environment with which a human user can interact.

Virus
A tiny organism that lives inside the cells·of animals, plants, and bacteria. Viruses can only reproduce inside cells and frequently cause diseases. In computing, a virus is a self-replicating computer program that often creates havoc by damaging other programs and erasing data in memory.

Webcasting
A system of broadcasting in which programs are played on websites, which listeners and viewers can access from their home computers via the Internet.

Website
Text, graphics, and other effects produced by a person or organization, and stored in a computer accessible to other computers via the Internet.

World Wide Web
The global network of interlinked websites, which can be accessed through the Internet.

WEBSITES

There are thousands of websites that relate to technology in our lives. Here are a few of them:

Scientific American is a well-respected journal that reveals important scientific breakthroughs and makes future predictions. To explore the future of transportation, medicine, weather prediction, and food production, visit the magazine's website at: http://www.sciam.com/

The magazine *Popular Science* examines the latest developments in technology and its impact. Its website can be found at: http://www.popsci.com

For information about robotics, which also includes links to other robot-related sites, try the NASA site at: http://www.robotics.jpl.nasa.gov/

For the latest news of developments in the world of computers, try the Computer Network CNET at: http://www.cnet.com/techtrends

MIT Labs have been at the forefront of machine and technology advances for decades. They publish an exciting and absorbing magazine called *Technology Review*. The online version can be accessed at: http://www.techreview.com/currnt.htm

For an interesting and thought-provoking collection of insights into what the future might bring for power, machinery, and the way we live in the middle of the 21st century, head over to *21st Century Creative Alternatives*. The website can be found at: http://web0.tiac.net/users/seeker/IT21stlinks.html

PLACES OF INTEREST

Many museums and science centers around the country have displays and exhibitions that highlight some of the latest and forthcoming developments in technology.

The National Air and Space Museum (Washington, D.C.) is part of the Smithsonian Institution. It has many galleries devoted to both the history of space flight and exploration, as well as exhibits and displays on what the future might bring.

The Museum of Science and Industry (Chicago, IL) is the oldest science museum in the Western hemisphere and the first in North America to have hands-on, interactive exhibits that explore all aspects of science and how it affects our lives.

The Space Center (Alamogordo, NM) celebrates all things related to space exploration. It aims to preserve and interpret the history, technology, and science of the Space Age.

The Computer Museum (Boston, MA) features a comprehensive history of computers that looks at their evolution, technology, and impact, as well as exhibits on robots and networks.

The California Science Center (Los Angeles, CA) features the *Creative World*, which examines how humans have built structures and machines to enhance their environment.

The Tech Musuem of Innovation (San Jose, CA) has over 240 interactive, hands-on exhibits about the technologies that affect our daily lives.

**The Cyberspace Museum of Natural History &
Exploration Technology** offers information on a variety of subjects, including space exploration. It can also point you toward other (real) museums that have related exhibitions. You can find it at: http://www.cyberspacemuseum.com

INDEX

ACKNOWLEDGMENTS

The publishers would like to thank the following illustrators for their contribution to this book:

Arcana, Julian Baum, Mike Buckley, Nik Clifford, Roger Harris, Richard Holloway, Graham Humphries, Dean McCallum, Alex Pang, Mark Preston, Real-Time Visualization

The publishers would like to thank the following for supplying the following photographs:

8 tl Slim Films, cl BT Laboratories, c GJLP – CNRI/SPL, bc Science Museum/Science & Society Picture Library; **8–9** c Tony Stone Worldwide/Ed Honowitz; **9** bl Science Museum/Science & Society Picture Library, bc (abacus) Science Museum/Science & Society Picture Library, bc Tony Stone Worldwide/Ed Honowitz, tr GJLP-CNRI/SPL, cr BT Laboratories; **10–11** t Science Museum/Science & Society Picture Library, b Science Museum/Science & Society Picture Library; **11** bl Science Museum/Science & Society Picture Library, bc AT & T Bell Labs/SPL, bcr Science Museum/Science & Society Picture Library, br Psion; **12** tl Tony Craddock/SPL, cr AT & T Bell Labs./SPL; **13** tl Popperfoto, tr Crown Copyright/Health & Safety Laboratories/SPL; **14** tl George Bernard/SPL, cl Popperfoto, c Rex Features/Nils Jorgensen, br Tony Stone Images/Mark Wagner; **15** t John Edward Linden/Arcaid, c BT Laboratories, cr The Advertising Archive, br George Bernard/SPL; **16** tl AKG London; **16–17** b C.S. Langlois, Publiphoto Diffusion/SPL, (background) Architects Design Partnership, London; **17** tl BT Laboratories, c George Haling/SPL, cr Popperfoto; **18** cl Apple Macintosh, cr Science Museum/Science & Society Picture Library, bc Hank Morgan/SPL; **19** tl BT Laboratories, br Powerstock/Zefa; **20–21** cr The Bridgeman Art Library, London; **21** tl British Museum/E.T. Archive; **22** bl The Advertising Archive, tc AKG/Bibliotheque Nationale, tr Palazzo Ducale, Mantua/AKG/Eric Lessing; **22–23** GJLP-CNRI/SPL; **23** tl Tony Stone Images/D.E. Cox, cr Hank Morgan/SPL; **24** tl Mary Evans Picture Library, tr NASA/Science & Society Picture Library, bl Dennis O'Claire /Tony Stone Images, bc Powerstock/Zefa, c Science Museum/Science & Society Picture Library, cr British Museum/E.T. Archive, br Roger Ressmeyer/Corbis; **25** bl Slim Films, c Science Museum/Science & Society Picture Library; **26** tl Peter Newark's Pictures, cl Corbis, bl Hulton Getty; **27** tl BT Archives, tc Science Museum/Science & Society Picture Library, bl BT Laboratories; **28** tl Hulton Getty, b UPI/Corbis-Bettmann, c Popperfoto, cr Tony Stone Images/Doug Armand; **29** tc Jonathon Blair/Corbis; **30** bl Paul Souders/Corbis, c Mary Evans Picture Library, br Mary Evans Picture Library; **30–31** Slim Films; **31** br BT Laboratories; **32** cl CERN photo, bl Corbis-Bettmann; **33** bc © Telehouse; **34** cl The Ronald Grant Archive, bc Popperfoto, c Robert Opie Collection, tc Christie's Images, tr The Ronald Grant Archive; **34–35** t Science Museum/Science & Society Picture Library; **35** cl Science Museum/Science & Society Picture Library, bl Corbis/Everett, all other pictures – Robert Opie Collection; **36** tl Rex Features, cr Image Bank/Steve Bronstein; **37** cl Peter Menzel/SPL, tr Electronic Arts, br Cyberlife, bc BT Laboratories; **38** tl SPL, bl John Howard/SPL, br Adrian Dennis/Rex Features; **39** tl C.S. Langlois, Publiphoto Diffusion/SPL; **40** tl Meliès/The Ronald Grant Archive, bl The Ronald Grant Archive; **40–41** The Ronald Grant Archive; **41** t The Bridgeman Art Library, London/ Stapleton Collection, tl IMAX; **42** tl Hulton Getty, cr Splash Communications Ltd; **42–43** b BT Laboratories; **43** tl IDEO, tr Philips Plasma; **44** tl BT Laboratories, tc Robert Opie Collection, c Dr Jurgen Scriba/SPL, bc Hulton Getty; **44–45** t John Frost Historical Newspaper Service, b Rex Features, tr BT Archives; **46** tl Hulton Getty, cr Popperfoto, bl BT Laboratories; **47** cr Corbis/UPI, bc Popperfoto; **48** cl Hulton Getty/G.Craddock, cr Rex Features/Nils Jorgensen, br Rex Features/Nils Jorgensen; **49** tl BT Laboratories, tr John Edward Linden/Arcaid, b BT Laboratories; **50** tr Tony Stone Images/Stewart Cohen, cl Mary Evans Picture Library, tr Rex Features/Patrick Barth, bl Tony Stone Images/Jon Riley; **50–51** Future Systems; **51** tr Tony Stone Images, cr Rex Features/Patrick Barth, br Tony Stone Images; **52** c (Meteosat Satellite) European Space Agency; **53** cl Jerry Mason/SPL, c Science Museum/Science & Society Picture Library; **54** tl Mary Evans Picture Library; **55** bl Philips, c Cybermotion, Inc.1998, cr INS/Brian Hatton; **56** tl Camera Press/Vario-Press, cl Rex Features/Peter Brooker, cr Corbis UK/Everett, bl Science Photo Library/David Ducros; **57** t The Aviation Picture Library/Austin J. Brown, cl CCS Communication Control System Ltd, bl Tony Stone Images/Chad Slattery, bc Tony Stone Images/Dennis O'Clair, br Tony Stone Images/Dennis O'Clair; **58** b Tony Stone Images/Ernest Braun, tc Science Museum/Science & Society Picture Library; **59** bl European Space Agency, c Nasa/SPL, tr Popperfoto/Reuter; **60** tl SPL/Novosti Press Agency, bl SPL/David Parker, br SPL/AT & T Bell Labs; **61** cl The Ronald Grant Archive/ Paramount Pictures, t Planet Earth Pictures, tr NASA/SPL; **62** tl Science Photo Library/600 Group Fanuc/David Parker, tr Sylvia Corday Photo Library Ltd, cl Mary Evans Picture Library, c Science & Society Picture Library/Science Museum, cr Hulton Getty (*car*), cr Science & Society Picture Library; **63** tl Xerox PARC/Dr K.Eric Drexler and Dr Ralph Merkle, tr Science Photo Library/Sam Ogden, cl Science Photo Library/Brian Brake; **64** tl The Bridgeman Art Library/Private Collection, bl Hulton Getty, c J.S.Automation; **65** tr Science Photo Library/Brian Brake, br Science Photo Library/Sam Ogden; **66** bl The Bridgeman Art Library/Private Collection; **67** t Science Photo Library/Peter Menzel, b The Ronald Grant Archive; **68** tl Science & Society Picture Library, tl Science Photo Library/Tony Craddock; **69** tl Institut fuer Mikrotechnik,Mainz GmbH, Germany, tr Science Photo Library/Manfred Kage; **70** tl Moorfields Eye Hospital, bl IBM, br Xerox PARC/DR K.Eric Drexler and Dr Ralph Merkle; **71** tl Science Photo Library/Ken Eward, tr Science Photo Library/Ken Eward, tc Science Photo Library/Ken Eward, cl Mary Evans Picture Library, br Tony Stone Images/Dennis O'Clair; **73** tl Science Photo Library/Eye of Science, bc Science Photo Library/Peter Menzel, br Science Photo Library/Ken Eward; **74** c Science Photo Library/Martin Bond, bl Science & Society Picture Library/Science Museum, br Mary Evans Picture Library; **76** cr Environmental Images/Martin Bond, tl Still Pictures/Herbert Giradet, cl Hutchinson Library/Dr Nigel Smith; **77** tl Science Photo Library/D.A.Peel; **78** tl Hulton Getty; **79** tl JET Joint Undertaking, cr Frank Spooner Pictures/Gamma-Liaison, bl Science Photo Library/Martin Bond, br Mary Evans Picture Library; **80** tl Camera Press/Ralph Crane, cl Science Photo Library/Martin Bond, cr Science Photo Library/Alex Bartel, br Honda (UK); **80–81** b Science Photo Library/Tommaso Guicciardini; **81** t Geoscience Features Picture Library; **82** tl The Bridgeman Art Library/Fitzwilliam Museum, University of Cambridge, cl Rex Features, bl Science Photo Library/David Parker; **83** tl Science Photo Library/Martin Bond; **84** tl Science & Society Picture Library/Science Museum/Clive Streeter, bl Frank Spooner Pictures/Gamma-Liaison; **84–85** c Science Photo Library/NASA, The Defence Picture Library, cl Rex Features/Dennis Cameron, tc (*bullet*) Jaycor, bc Rex Features/Dennis Cameron, bl SPAWAR, br Science & Society Picture Library/Science Fiction FNDTN; **87** cl Frank Spooner Pictures/Charles/Liaison, (*Satellite*) Camera Press/Ray Hamilton, cl NASA, cr Diners Club International, (*Sputnik*) Science Photo Library/Novosti; **88** c Frank Spooner Pictures/Liaison, bl Philips/Visions of the Future; **89** cr Softroom/Design: J.Jones/ T.Spencer, b /Design: J.Jones/ T.Spencer, **90** tl Frank Spooner Pictures/Gamma-Liaison, cl Science Photo Library/Hank Morgan, **91** tc Mary Evans Picture Library, cr Science Photo Library/Hank Morgan, br Science Photo Library/Peter Yates; **92** tc Hulton Getty; c Frank Spooner Pictures/Gamma-Liaison; **93** tr Frank Spooner Pictures/Gamma-Liaison, c Science Photo Library/ Jerrican Daudier; **94** tl Science Photo Library/Spencer Grant, cl Science Photo Library/Hank Morgan, b BNFL; **95** t Frank Spooner Pictures/FSP/Gamma/Tom Kidd, b NASA Ames Research Center; **96** tl Mary Evans Picture Library; **97** tr Frank Spooner Pictures/Gamma-Liaison, cr Frank Spooner Pictures/Gamma-Liaison; **98** tr Lockheed Martin, cl Science Photo Library/NASA, b NASA; **99** b Science Photo Library/Victor Habbick Visions; **100** tl Science Photo Library/NASA, cl Science Photo Library/NASA, cr Science Photo Library/NASA, bl Science Photo Library/David Ducros, bc Science Photo Library/David Ducros; **102** tl Science Photo Library; **103** tc Science Photo Library/Peter Menzel**104** c Hulton Getty, cr Arcaid/Richard Bryant, bl Hulton Getty; **106** tl Mary Evans Picture Library, cl Science Photo Library/David Parker, bl Science Photo Library/M-Sat Ltd; **107** tc Science Photo Library/David Nunuk; **108** tl Mary Evans Picture Library, bc Still Pictures/Shehzad Nooran; **109** t Frank Spooner Pictures/Gamma, cr Arcaid/Ian Lambot, bc Mary Evans Picture Library; **110** tl Hulton Getty, bl Science Photo Library/George Olson; **111** TR Environmental Images/Martin Bond, br Frank Spooner Pictures/Gamma; **113** t Science & Society Picture Library/Louis Hine/NMPFT, Bradford, cl Science Photo Library/David Parker, cr Science Photo Library/John Mead, br Frank Spooner Pictures/Auenturier; **114** l Mary Evans Picture Library, c Mary Evans Picture Library, cr Science & Society Picture Library/Science Museum, r Rex Features; **115** l Rex Features, cl Rex Features, cr Quadrant Picture Library; **116** tl Hulton Getty, br Rex Features/Peter Brooker; **116–117** c Rex Features; **117** tr Ford Motor Company, cr Quadrant Picture Library, br Vin Mag Archive Ltd; **118** t Hulton Getty, c Mercedes-Benz; **119** tl Rex Features, tr Rex Features, c Rex Features/Nils Jorgensen, b Frank Spooner Pictures/Gamma Liaison; **120** t The Bridgeman Art Library/British Library; **121** t Solar Sailor, tl Rex Features, cl Tony Stone Images/Alastair Black, bc Rex Features, br Colorific/Paul Van Riel/Black Star; **122** tr Vin Mag Archive Ltd, bc Rex Features; **123** c British Airways, br Dennis Gilbert; **124** tl TRH, c Frank Spooner Pictures; **125** l Science Photo Library/Marshall Space Flight Center/NASA, r Martin Breeze/Retrograph Archive Ltd; **126** cl Science & Society Picture Library/Daily Herald Archive/NMPFT, c Rex Features, cr Rex Features, r Science & Society Picture Library/Science Museum; **128** tl Mary Evans Picture Library, bl Rex Features/Simon Hadley, bc Science Photo Library/Sam Ogden; **129** tl Tony Stone Images/Wayne R Bilenduke, bl Science Photo Library/James King-Holmes, br Rex Features; **130** tl Mary Evans Picture Library, cr Tony Stone Images/Walter Hodges, bl John Walmsely, BR Science Photo Library/Blair Seitz; **131** tr Camera Press/Stewart Mark; **132** tl Mary Evans Picture Library, cl Telegraph Colour Library/Jose Azel/Aurora; **133** tr Robert Harding Picture Library/Bill O'Connor, c Robert Harding Picture Library/Geoff Renner, br Planet Earth Pictures/Gary Bell; **134** tl Mary Evans Picture Library, bl Frank Spooner Pictures/Gamma presse images; **135** tl Allsport/Sylvain Cazenave, cr Katz Pictures/George Steinmetz/National Geographic Society; bc Rex Features; br Rex Features, **136** tl Mary Evans Picture Library/Barry Norman Collection, bl Allsport/Anne-Marie Weber; **136–137** c Rex Features, **137** tr Allsport/Didier Givois, br Allsport/Simon Bruty; **138** cr Science Photo Library/Laguna Design; **139** l Rex Features, cl Science & Society Picture Library/Science Museum, c Mary Evans Picture Library, br Science & Society Picture Library/Science Museum; **140** tl Mary Evans Picture Library, cl Rex Features/Pierre Schwartz/Sipa Press, bl Science Photo Library/Novosti Press Agency, br Science Photo Library/Simon Fraser; **141** tr Science Photo Library/David Ducros; **142** tr Hulton Getty, cl Still Pictures/Michel Roggo, cr Robert Harding Picture Library, b Still Pictures/Mark Edwards; **143** tl Still Pictures/Peter Frischmuth, tr Mary Evans Picture Library, b Science Photo Library/Peter Menzel; **144** c Science Photo Library/Tek Image; **145** tr Commonwealth Scientific and Industrial Research Organisation, c Science Photo Library/Tommaso Guicciardini; **146** tl Science Photo Library/A.Barrington Brown, c Science Photo Library/Makoto/Eurelios, bl Rex Features/Jeremy Sutton Hibbert, br Science Photo Library/Peter Menzel; **147** tl Still Pictures/Robert Holmgren, tr Science Photo Library/Laguna Design, c Science Photo Library/Peter Yates; **148** tl Mary Evans Picture Library, bl Science Photo Library/Simon Fraser; **149** tl Science Photo Library/Barry Dowsett, cl Science Photo Library/Simon Fraser, cr Science Photo Library/Geoff Tompkinson; **150** tr Mary Evans Picture Library/Webber, 1815, cl Science Photo Library/J.C. Revy, c BBC Photographic Library/Tomorrow's World, br Science Photo Library/Geoff Tompkinson; **151** tr Science Photo Library/Klaus Guldbrandsen, bl Rex Features; **152** tl Mary Evans Picture Library; **153** tl Science Photo Library/James King-Holmes, tr Still Pictures/Adrian Arbib, ctr Frank Spooner Pictures/Gamma Liaison.

Key: b = bottom, c = center, l=left, t = top, r = right

Every effort has been made to trace the copyright holders of the photographs. The publishers apologize for any inconvenience caused.

The publishers would like to thank the following: Kate Amy, Preston Carter, Martin Cross, Sinead Derbyshire, Keith Goodall of Stantec, Andy Gower, Cormac Jordan, Robert Kemp, Malcolm Lee, Gerhardt Meurer of Johns Hopkins University, William Murray, Ian Pearson, Dr. Andrew Rudge of BNFL, Michael White, and Danny Wooton.